THE NEBRASKA DISPATCHES

CHRISTOPHER
CARTMILL
>> THE NEBRASKA
DISPATCHES

UNIVERSITY OF NEBRASKA PRESS
LINCOLN & LONDON

Publication of this volume was assisted by
The Virginia Faulkner Fund, established in
memory of Virginia Faulkner, editor in chief
of the University of Nebraska Press.

Library of Congress Cataloging-in-Publication
Data
Cartmill, Christopher.
The Nebraska dispatches / Christopher
Cartmill.
p. cm.
ISBN 978-0-8032-2294-6 (cloth : alk. paper)
1. Nebraska—Drama. 2. One-person shows
(Performing arts) I. Title.
PS3603.A79125N43   2010
812'.6—dc22
2010009620

To Joyce and Renée—strong souls and loving mothers.

>>Acknowledgments

The author wishes to thank Christine Marie Brown, Eva Rubinstein, Virginia Lowery, the Omaha Nation, the Ponca Nation, the Santee Nation, the Winnebago Nation, Charles Bethea, Nancy Engen-Wedin, Amy Ossian, Rachael Cassidy, Michelle Kiefel, the Lied Center for the Performing Arts, Sara Keene, the Kramer Family, Kathleen O'Grady, Alice Dittman, Ellen Baldwin, Glenn Smith, Adam Langer, Barbara Hammond, Carol Svoboda, Gina Klein, Dianne and Walker Kennedy, Sally Desmond, Alice Saunsoci, Elsie Clark, the Kimmel Harding Nelson Center, Andrés Fagundez, the Center for Great Plains Studies, Judi gaiashkibos, Christine Lesiak, Joe Starita, Bill Achord, John Mangan, Eleanor Baxter, Carol Svoboda, Stuart and Kelli Kerns, Dan C. Jones, Ladette Randolph, Tom Swanson, Heather Lundine, Ann Baker, Brenda Wyers, Randall Ksionzek, Jeff Malan, the University of Nebraska Foundation, Dick Hatfield, Kate and Peter McGovern, Jeff Korbelik, Michelle Baker, Mary Sue Glosser, Donny Epstein, Jeff Larson, Julie Evan Smith, Marge Royce, Jennifer Roszell, Alycia Smith-Howard Timmis, John Wright, Ken Bolden, Marco Aurélio Maximo Prado, Joe Schulz, Richard Ende, Jennifer Wise, Carol and Scott Miller, Meredith Miller, Courtney Miller, Randy and Cindy Cartmill, Craig and Mauria Cartmill, Rowen and Jonas and Allison Cartmill.

And a very special thanks to Laura Kendall and Laura J. Sweet.

New York City, New York

These dispatches are taken from a series of emails sent to family and friends during the almost three-year process of writing and researching a new play. The play is done. It is titled *Home Land*. But it is only one part of a deeply personal journey. These dispatches are fragments of that journey, of my still-growing awareness, of a creative process, and of an understanding of the power of place and the power of the past. The events are true. The names of the living are changed. The signs were there. All weather portrayed was real.

So, like another more famous odyssey begins: Speak to me, Spirits, and through me tell a story of home. Wait. This is my home, this is our home—isn't it?

>>DISPATCH: A STORY OF MY PARENTS
A Hazardous Attempt at Autobiographical Context

I remember when I was a kid thinking that the house we lived in was on top of an enormous hill. At the time we lived in a part of Kansas where there are no hills. That's what memory does.

While other kids' houses smelled of beef barley soup, our house glowed with the scent of whiskey and Miss Dior. My father was a handsome self-made man from the southern great plains who had been something of a ne'er-do-well in school— caring more for golf than education. That is, until he married my mother. She was a part-time model and self-made woman of great energy and beauty and education. Her passions were for the theater, for teaching, and for my father.

Robert Samuel Cartmill was a grain merchant. When I explain that my family moved around a lot while I was growing up, most assume I was a military brat. My brother and sister and I grew up following the harvest, literally and figuratively. For a couple of years we lived in hotels as my father worked his way up to becoming an important figure in the industry, to this day remembered and respected by those who worked with and for him.

Everywhere we lived my mother made it a home. She had a magic energy. She made it appear, to everyone around, that we had been living in each place for years. Not only were all boxes unpacked in a matter of hours, but we were embraced by the community and treated like natives within weeks of our arrival. Joyce Ellen Cartmill had glamour, yes, but also a charm that made everyone feel as a truly treasured friend.

By the time I came around, my parents had seemingly lost interest in photographic documentation. There are only a handful of pictures of me in early childhood, and almost all are the same: usually my brother is in a sporty, crisp suit, my sister is in a sweet little dress and shiny shoes, and I am in nothing but my underpants. There's me standing by a birdfeeder—in my underpants. There's me on an Easter morning—in my underpants. There's me at my father's side near the Christmas tree—in my underpants. There's me playing what seems to be a game of Cowboys-and-Indians— in my underpants. My mother told me many pictures got lost in one of our moves.

I felt distinctly out of place most of the time. Only two things fascinated me: playing at theater and observing all the interesting people my parents entertained. I would stage plays and monologues for family and guests and sometimes had to be restrained in my enthusiasm for telling stories. I loved making them and hearing them. On one extraordinary evening I sat at the end of our long dining table while a Japanese associate of my father's told his story of being a kamikaze pilot who never took off. Just as his squadron was getting set to take off, he told us, the end of the war was declared. He was just one interesting person among many.

My father was never keen on my theatrical interest. "Acting is for the flighty and the neurotic," he once told me. "You're not that. But you'll do what you must. Whatever you do, son, you'd better do it to the best of your abilities— nothing by half and no mediocrity. You come from better people than that." The artists he respected most were writers. I started writing while he was sick, working on what eventually became my first play.

My father didn't live to see it produced or to know me as a writer. My mother took my hand on the opening night of that play when it premiered in Chicago and said, "It's nothing by half." It certainly wasn't. My first play was a six-hour epic about the French Revolution. My mother never missed a performance or an opening night of it, no matter when or where. She worked very hard to understand my work, not just support it. She became an artistic home for me.

>>Dispatch: Home

August 1979. Lincoln, Nebraska

My family's home, when we first moved to Lincoln, was on the last street in the city, officially. To the south and west was an undulating expanse of corn, soybean, and wheat fields. Now, from that same house urban development stretches as far as the eye can see. Home is a constantly changing thing, I guess. Growing up, home was indeed a changing thing. I was born in southern Kansas near the

Oklahoma border, but my family lived in seven places before I turned seventeen.

I was on a school trip when my parents moved us from the place I loved the most during our family's nomadic life—the wooded river city of Memphis, Tennessee—to our new home on the edge of the horizon. On the evening when I arrive to be introduced to my new home, I am greeted by massive billows of charcoal-colored clouds that roll in and devour the western twilight. A storm like no storm I had ever known before seems to surround us. The house shakes, and rips of lightning tear down and across the sky. Welcome to the Heartland. Welcome home.

According to the teachings of a people who came to this land ages ago, before there was a Nebraska to be made my home, this storm, like all others, is the work of the Thunderbirds. Thunderbirds are part of the Great Spirit. Their power protects and destroys; it is good and bad. It's also believed that certain stories come from the thunder—stories of honor, but also of shame. Speak those stories and the earth shakes. A story brings you power, I am told, but you do have to pay for it.

>>Dispatch: A Very Brief Geography and Eurocentric History of Nebraska

Where the West Begins

Out where the handclasp's a little stronger,
Out where the smile dwells a little longer,
That's where the West begins . . .

—Excerpt of poem by Arthur Chapman, 1917

In case you're wondering, the exact place where the handclasp is stronger and the smile is longer, it is the intersection of 13th and "O" streets in Lincoln, Nebraska. Truly. There is a large brick star to mark it. And if you want to find where the West begins: Nebraska is a state bordered by Iowa to the east; Missouri to the southeast; Kansas to the south; Colorado to the southwest; Wyoming to the northwest; and South Dakota to the north.

For millions of years Nebraska was underwater—and home to nautiloids, squid, and octopuses. When the Rocky Mountains began to rise up to the west, everything dried out and the dinosaurs died out. But before it all got too settled, the Great Ice Age scoured in and roughed up the place. Woolly mammoths, rhinoceroses, and pigs seven feet high shared the land with a relative newcomer, humans. As the glaciers retreated they left the eastern part of the land—near the Missouri River—rubbed, dented, and caressed into gentle hills and scenic bluffs. Going west the landscape transitions into the Sandhills and then the High Plains.

> Out where the skies are a trifle bluer,
> Out where friendship's a little truer,
> That's where the West begins . . .

Nebraska seems to have gotten its name from an indigenous word for "flat water," likely a reference to the Platte River that runs through the state. Europeans considered this land part of what they called "The Great American Desert." They didn't mean it had a landscape exactly like the Gobi or the Sahara. The word "desert" comes from the Latin "desertum," meaning simply "an abandoned place."

Before the mid-nineteenth century the plains had been abandoned to the Indians, many of whom had been pressed from the east. But in 1854 the Nebraska-Kansas Act created the Kansas and Nebraska territories. It was all a part of trying to keep the country from the precipice of the unavoidable that was the Civil War. The act gave settlers in the territories the right to decide if they wanted to allow slavery within their borders. Kansas became the bloody battleground for the mess Congress had created. During the 1860s, and despite the controversy, settlers poured into the territories to claim free land offered by the government. The majority of the settlers—homesteaders—were foreign born: Germans, Swedes, Irish, English, Czech.

Nebraska was made the 37th state of the Union just after the Civil War came to an end. The state capital was moved to Lincoln, an outpost formerly known as Lancaster but renamed in honor of the beloved dead president. By 1870 the population of the state was numbered at 122,993. As of 2008, the population was estimated at 1,783,432, which is only about 100,000 less than the same year's estimation of the population of the island of Manhattan.

When I tell people who don't know the place about Nebraska they will invariably say something like, "Oh, I drove through there once." It's as though the state motto should be "Nebraska, the Way to Get to Colorado." Nebraska is more than a liminal experience. It is the Heartland. Nebraska gave us Arbor Day, CliffsNotes, Willa Cather (though originally a Virginian), the Union Pacific Railway, Henry Fonda, Johnny Carson, Warren Buffett, and the Vise-Grip. Good representatives of a place that's growing, impatient, novel, standard gauge, wryly humorous, entrepreneurial, and practical. Kool-Aid was invented in Nebraska and is still the official soft drink of the state. No other state in the Union has an official soft drink—though it should be noted that the official state "beverage" is milk. Nebraskans are mad for football—University of Nebraska football. Memorial Stadium, on the campus of the University in Lincoln, can and does hold more than twice the population of the state's third largest city. On game days it is a giant bowl of the color red that I am certain can be seen and perhaps heard from space. Nebraska teaches that we should never be deceived by the seeming uniformity. The place has its singularities. Nebraska is the only state in the country with a unicameral legislature, meaning a single house. It doesn't make the politics any better, it just puts it all in one room. Nebraska is politically conservative and yet has a history of activism and reform. One of the first national chapters of the NAACP was established in Omaha in 1912. The state motto is "Equality Before the Law," but for many years the state slogan was "Nebraska, The Good Life." For many it's a good place to call home.

> Where there's more of singing and less of sighing,
> Where there's more of giving and less of buying,
> And a man makes friends without half trying—
> That's where the West begins.

>>DISPATCH: TWO RIVERS, TWO RAINBOWS, AND ONE BEGINNING
Friday, August 16, 2002. Niobrara, Nebraska

A sudden storm blows through and hail comes down like it's being thrown. My mother and I take shelter under the bullhorns and antelope heads of the Two Rivers Wild West Saloon, Gas Station, and Hotel. We'd come up the 4½ hours to Niobrara from Lincoln for the annual Ponca Tribal pow-wow. You see, for some inexplicable reason I had gotten it into my head that this was something I needed to do, and my mother wanted to come. My mother often said "yes" to adventure.

There among the antlers I see, in a place of honor all its own, a single large photo of a noble Native chief wrapped in a blanket, wearing a single black-tipped eagle feather. I know he has a story to tell.

Soon it stops hailing but the wind's up. As we drive into the Ponca Agency the sky opens up to blue and the sun comes down as if it's being thrown. A high double rainbow arches over the fences to the east. Later I am told by a Native friend and teacher that the rainbow was a sign—a sign that we were supposed to be there. A promise. I also found out the identity of that Indian chief: the famous Chief Standing Bear of the Ponca Tribe.

Not famous to you? Some will tell you the story simply: Standing Bear was a man who lost his home and won it back.

>>DISPATCH: HOME AGAIN
Four Years Later. July 2006

My father is gone. My mother is gone. She died in her own bed three years earlier to the month, surrounded by her children and grandchildren. Since that time I've been losing my connection to the home I had known in Nebraska. I can no longer go to the house where my father toasted my mother on their last anniversary just before he died, almost twenty years ago. My stepfather estranged himself from me by remarrying only a few months after my mother's death. Many days I feel it's easier just to let my Nebraska connections go. But I have a commission for a new play, a commission from the Lied Center for the Performing Arts. I'm to tell the story of Chief Standing Bear. I am to go back to Nebraska for a month to work on the play

and, ostensibly, to get the blessing of the Native community. How naive I am in so many ways. How naive I am to
think I couldn't possibly come home a stranger.

>>Dispatch: My Nebraska

July 31, 2006. Lincoln, Nebraska. Temperature: 105°

First things first. Car. I don't have a car in New York City.
I walk. In Nebraska you walk for exercise, not for transit.
It's not just a matter of distance. It's psychological. The Lied
Center has made an arrangement with a local car dealer-
ship. I'm dropped off at the car lot and see my "deal": a little black Aveo. I remember thinking, "Aveo. Aveo. It could
be an Indian name: *Aveo.*" My trusty steed—my very tiny
trusty steed. On the highway, the wind from semi trucks
can and does blow me onto the shoulder of the road. But
it is acceptance at first sight.

*The Same Day, 5:00 p.m. Madonna Rehabilitation
Hospital, Lincoln*

I have a family visit to make. Deb Steinkolk is the daughter of Alma Kisker, who was my mother's maid for twenty-three years. Deb has had a mysterious and rapid onset
of multiple sclerosis—from symptoms to coma in ten days.
Deb has just been brought out of intensive care. She is par-
alyzed from the neck down and can speak only about one
word at a time. Deb knows my name and keeps repeating it. I'm pretty certain her mother prompted her. But before I leave, to Alma's amazement and clearly unprompted,
Deb starts repeating "The Way Home." *The Way Home.*
"*The Way Home*" is another play of mine, one that Deb
had been a part of when we produced it in Lincoln years
before. *The Way Home.* She starts to cry, even though her

face is immobile. Deb has two kids. One is fifteen months old. Deb is twenty-five.

That Evening

I am staying with my high school drama teacher. Her place is directly across the street from the house that had been my family home for seventeen years. In the summer evening heat I sit on the hood of the little black Aveo for a moment and look for any life that may be going on in my old home. I realize what a large task I have set for myself. The story of Standing Bear is powerful and large in so many ways. And personal. But why? What does this man and his journey have to do with me?

I have made it clear to the Lied Center staff that in order to do this properly I need to meet as many people as possible in the Native community and in the broader Nebraska community—before I write. I want to interview all sorts of people. I don't want to write a history pageant. I don't know what I want to write, specifically, but I want the work to have meaning now—meaning for the present. I want to strive for authenticity.

>>DISPATCH: AUTHENTICITY
Sometime in the Late to Middle 1990s

When I first move to New York City I am invited to a reading of a play. The playwright has the prophetically pretentious name of Ileana Bordeaux. Ileana Bordeaux has been given a large grant. She has spent a profitable two whole weeks in Nebraska. She certainly has taken ownership of her subject, because Ileana Bordeaux returns to New York City and pens what she calls a "deconstruction" of Willa Cather's *My Antonia*. She titles the play *My Nebraska*.

Okay, but if it's *her* Nebraska, why did she have to borrow it from Willa Cather? I can certainly say it isn't *my* Nebraska. At the performance of it I writhe in my seat, listening and getting angrier and angrier, then it comes to me that by "deconstruction" Ileana Bordeaux actually means an arrogant, acquisitive, and unimaginative "redecorating." Tart it up with clichés and paper it with shallow understandings. Rearrange the furniture and say you've built the house. Take a story and make it your own. That's not writing; that's conquest. But whose Nebraska is it?

>>DISPATCH: RESIDENCY

August 8, 2006. The Kimmel Harding Nelson Center for the Arts, Nebraska City, Nebraska

Nebraska City is on the southeast edge of the state, on the banks of the Missouri. The center is a retreat for artists. I was the first writer invited to stay, just weeks after my mother died. I intended to write and research but I couldn't concentrate. I grieved. I have arranged to stay here again and use Nebraska City as my base for the month. I have my own office and studio overlooking the old brick streets of Nebraska City.

I have my resource books with me. My research: *An Unspeakable Sadness: The Dispossession of the Nebraska Indians* by David Wishart; *The Omaha Tribe* by Alice C. Fletcher and Francis LaFlesche; and *Buckskin and Blanket Days* by T. H. Tibbles. I've also brought with me a copy of a photograph that my uncle gave me. It is a picture of a woman with piercing eyes—my great-great grandmother. My uncle has told me she was a full-blooded Native, likely Sioux, perhaps Cherokee. He doesn't know yet. So much is recorded of my family's history but this is a piece of which little is known. Her name seems to have been written on the photograph but is unreadable now. I don't know what, if anything, she has to do with this work.

>>DISPATCH: HE'DEWACHI

Saturday, August 12. Temperature: 102°

I have driven the north-south width of Nebraska four times in two weeks. Attended the Omaha He'dewachi (essentially, powwow) in Macy, Nebraska. The Aveo and I are dribbled like a basketball all the way to the toll bridge at Decatur—"Proud to be Nebraska's Second Oldest Settlement," an ironic slogan for a town that lies just outside an Indian reservation.

Walking down to the powwow grounds I'm a little self-conscious. Wanting not to look like the cultural tourist I am, I went and bought a pair of boots—kick-ass boots. I got me some style and a hitch in my gitty-up. I think I look either very cool or like a reenactor from Decatur's Second Settlement Riverfront Days.

I am supposed to meet up with Susann Cloud Horse, whom I had met the week before in the company of her children. I accept that our meeting will happen in its own time—Indian time. It's like the clocks that say "Indian Time" that can be found for sale at the Lincoln powwow: no numbers, just free roaming hands.

I should just take in the fullness. And it is full.

Hundreds of people are moving clockwise around the powwow grounds. The sacred circle. As far as I understand, this placement is the same as that once used for the arrangement of the teepees on the annual buffalo hunts and mirrors the setup of the earth lodges back at the permanent settlement. The entrance is always at the east, the direction of the rising sun. During the *he'dewachi* the dais for the tribal leaders and other dignitaries is at the west— a place they would take in the earth lodge. At the center of the ring is both a pole, or tree, and a tent for the host drum. The host drum is a group from the local tribe. Other drum circles sit around the edges of the circle in a pattern that is based on their affiliations. There are bleachers for tourists all around the arena, but most of the "relatives" (those of Native descent) are sitting in lawn chairs of a kind that you get used to seeing at powwows.

The circle is full. The drumming and singing is amplified. The sounds are countered by the running commentary of a master of ceremonies, which in this case is "Chiefie." The emcee's ongoing monologue is fascinating: part tradition police and part day-time talk show host.

The powwow grounds are filled with dancers in their regalia. That's the proper word for the colorful, be-feathered, beaded, and tasseled dancing clothes. There are tail dancers, fancy dancers, shawl dancers, grass dancers, jingle dancers, and traditionally dressed women of all ages. Many are dancing without regalia. Everyone has his or her colors or mixes of colors. It's a beautiful sight.

Susann is not the first to find me. Martin Cloud Horse, Susann's six-year-old son, finds me first. He has a great grin that extends literally from one ear to the other and a child's lisp he undoubtedly will grow out of.

Martin looks you right in the eye and could force a smile from a rock. When we meet he tells me he's been following me for a while. He's practicing, he says, his sneaking. I ask him where his mother is and he points out to the dancers. She is dancing with her mother, Elise, and youngest daughter, Jewel. Susann and Jewel are not in regalia, but they are in pink. Susann's mother is in a traditional dress of blue with large intricate matching beadwork medallions attached to her long braids. The women's dance is an elegant and subtle step walk. The three generations are all holding hands.

When I turn around, Martin has disappeared (obviously practicing more sneaking) and is replaced by his older brother, Valdis. Valdis is a husky, sensitive, melancholy kid of eight. He's got years of sadness in his eyes. Valdis doesn't say anything, just looks at me and runs off. I get a tap on my shoulder. It's Sophie, Susann's eldest. Sophie is eleven, tall and quick.

Susann takes a break and wants to get out of the sun so we go to sit on the bleachers near the entrance to the powwow grounds to watch the dancing and talk. Martin practices sneaking through the bleachers and smiles at me when I catch him with my eyes.

Susann has had a tough year. She had some health problems and her husband of fourteen years abruptly left her and the kids. Susann is radiant and tall, like her daughter, Sophie, and formidable, like her mother. We sit half-listening to the speeches of the candidates for Powwow Princess. Chiefie is introducing each candidate and handing the microphone to each, who make candid statements of purpose. I catch a bit of a candidate's speech: "I don't do drugs or alcohol. I won't do like others may. I walk my faith and tradition."

Susann explains to me that this year has been a tough one for the Omaha—a rash of suicides among young people on the reservation. One suicide took place just the week before—and a murder the week before that. Drug and alcohol problems are epidemic, as are abuse and neglect. At some point Sophie and Martin nestle close between Susann and me. Sophie shows me her vampire impression, which looks a lot like an English butler with an overbite, as she holds a clutch purse with both hands. Five-year-old Jewel laughingly jumps on Sophie with muddy hands. Martin chimes in that he's going to be Superman for Halloween. Valdis is nowhere in sight.

"I love my people. I won't disappoint my family by doing bad things. I want to make them proud." So says the final candidate for "Powwow Princess," holding an eagle-feather fan and wearing a high beaded crown and glasses. Susann goes off to check on her mother. Sophie stays sitting close. Martin grabs hold of my boots. And the question sweeps over me like the wind: "Who am I, really, in all this? I, with my jeans and just-bought boots?"

>>DISPATCH: EUGENE
Late Afternoon of the Same Day

Martin can predict the weather. Sophie tells me so while we're tossing a beach ball by the tent Susann's family has set up. Sophie lets the ball drop and says, "Martin, is it going to thunderstorm tomorrow?"

Martin stands stock still, stares off into some imagined horizon, then smiles and nods and runs to get the beach ball. Susann laughs and says that it's true. Then she motions me to follow her. Susann wants to introduce me around.

Her cousin Eugene is the first on her list. Eugene is a tail dancer. She points him out. He is dressed in a black and white shirt with appliqué silhouettes of buffalo skulls on the arms and chest. He has a horsehair bonnet topped with two eagle feathers and a big Sioux-style eagle feather bustle. And glasses. Susann says we should go over to him before he goes back into the dance. Eugene is standing drinking an Aquafina with another dancer, who is wearing Day-Glo orange. The other man is quite short and a fellow tail dancer. Susann introduces me to Eugene. "This is Christopher Cartmill," says Susann simply.

Pause.

"Cart-what?" Eugene asks with the flat downward inflection I am getting very used to.

"Cart-mill. He's a playwright. He's from New York City. Working on the Standing Bear story," says Susann who, I think, sees that I'm at a loss. But she is willing to help me only so much.

Silence.

"You're a playwright."

Pause.

"I'm a playwright."

"You're a playwright."

Silence, during which Eugene takes a swig from the bottle. "So. What do you do?"

Pause.

"I write plays."

Silence.

Eugene's friend laughs and looks at me. He shakes his head. I'm assuming he'll be excited to see the play written by the articulate playwright from New York City—the new Beckett. The conversation stumbles along for about five minutes more. What interests me is that the stories Eugene knows about Standing Bear (who was from a different, though related, tribe) I have not found in any of the books I have used in researching the chief. Eugene's stories seem to be at odds with the historical facts.

"Standing Bear. Five horses were shot out from under him by the white men in battle," Eugene tells me.

"Really? But . . . we . . . Never mind. I . . ."

Eugene's friend and fellow tail dancer wants nothing to do with our conversation. I feel out of my element. Before I can get even more confused and tongue-tied they both step into the dance. Susann motions me to follow her. She wants to introduce me to her aunt. Along the way, she looks at me with a sparkle in her eye and says, "Nice boots. You just need the cowboy hat to make it perfect."

>>Dispatch: Testing

The Same Evening. 6:00 p.m.

We don't find Susann's aunt. But Susann is participating in an intertribal run from the Rosebud Reservation in South Dakota to the he'dewachi in Macy, Nebraska. Rosebud, South Dakota, is toward the panhandle side of Nebraska, so this is a goodly run. It's been organized to support youth organizations and education—to raise awareness and prevention of youth suicide, addiction, abuse, and violence. Susann has been looking forward to the run for months and was the Omaha reservation representative on the organizing committee. Her job is to meet the runners in Vermillion, South Dakota.

I have no idea where Vermillion is. I just agreed to drive her because that gives us time to talk. We planned to leave around 5:00 p.m., which would give me plenty of time to drive the little Aveo all the way back down the Missouri to Nebraska City before dawn.

While waiting for Susann, I wander the grounds. I ask a young woman with lovely eyes and a particularly authentic-looking regalia if I could take her picture. She tells me simply, "No."

I look at the artwork being sold at a booth filled with non-Natives from Santa Fe. I almost buy a t-shirt. Then the evening round of dancing begins. The drums are giving a roll call. The tail dancers start. I observe some Mormon missionaries eating what's called a Walking Taco, which is a potato chip bag filled with chips and heaped with beef and cheese. They eat with a missionary zeal.

Finally I see Susann moving through the tents. She's speaking to a smallish woman in black. She waves me over. She wants to introduce me to her aunt. Finally. But I'm considering my ride from somewhere up in the unknown of South Dakota to Nebraska City. I'm considering the fact that I'll be sleeping in my car somewhere outside Sioux City, Iowa. Still, I agree to meet Aunt Marguerite.

Marguerite Baker holds the most powerful female position on the reservation—the first-ever female tribal chairwoman. She is much more excited to meet me than anyone I've met so far. She thinks I'm a filmmaker. Even when Susann and I correct her she insists that she can't wait to see my film. Suddenly, a frail, wrinkled man rolls up in a beaten-up old electric wheelchair. His head is tilted to his left and hangs there with effort. "I want you to meet my eldest brother, Albert," Marguerite says, as she stops his wheelchair with her foot and leans down right to his ear.

"ALBERT, THIS MAN MAKES MOVIES! HE'S MAKING A MOVIE ABOUT STANDING BEAR!"

"Is he?"

"Yes, sir. I have been working with the Lied Center and have a—"

"What's he saying? What?!"

"Uncle Albert is a little hard of hearing."

"Noise. Too much noise!" Uncle Albert says as he rolls away from his younger sister.

"You should speak with him. He knows everything about the old days. WOULD YOU LIKE TO SPEAK TO HIM, ALBERT?"

"Not here. Too much noise! Come on!"

I look over at Susann, knowing that she has to meet up with some folks who've run half of South Dakota and will have a sizeable chunk of Nebraska still to run, and I will have to drive back from wherever we're going. Already we're almost two hours behind the schedule I had in my head. But this is a chance I might never have again. Susann shrugs as if to say, "The choice is yours." She smiles and laughs, I think because I look so worried about everything but where I am. I am not being present.

"Too noisy! Come on!" With that, Uncle Albert shoots across the dirt path and leaves Susann and me scurrying after him. He keeps talking while he rolls in-between parked and moving cars. He darts between two vans. I'm behind him by about two steps, wondering if I should grab the handles. But before I can even touch them Uncle Albert abruptly turns right and shoots up a small hill. "Up here! Not so much noise!"

He shoves himself in-between vans and gets caught on an Escalade's trailer hitch.

"Do you need any help, sir?"

"What?!" He puts on the gas and the right wheel spins in the mud. I reach for the handles, thinking to lift him up and off the hitch. "I'm fine!" And with that, he pops off the hitch and skids up into a white tent at the edge of the grounds.

"Here's a place for you to sit."

I sit and don't know what to say. Susann is waiting. Uncle Albert is waiting.

"If *you're* not going to talk, I will. My grandfather knew him, Standing Bear. They were Ponca. We let them come here. Like the Winnebago. No place to go."

"Sir, your hospitality as a nation is famous."

"Gets us into trouble, though."

I look again to Susann. Nothing. This is my show. I notice how dirty Albert's white t-shirt is, how everything about him leans to the right. How dark his skin is. How the wrinkles around his smile let me know he likes to laugh. How his eyes sparkle like obsidian.

"Standing Bear. Five horses were shot out from under him by the white men in battle."

The same thing Eugene had said, but as far as I know, as far as any historian has told me, as far as I have read of Standing Bear's own statements, Standing Bear never fought against the American military or any settlers. I think it would be disrespectful to question Uncle Albert on this point and, anyway, what the hell do I know? What do historians really know? So I say, "Tell me, sir, about what this place was like before?"

"Beautiful land. Beautiful land. The Mandan were here before us. They're gone. The others were sent off but we stayed. The treaties let us stay. We were smart. Not so smart to let the Winnebago come here. But the government lied, like they lied to the others."

He goes on and I don't understand what I hear. I can't think. I nod and ask other questions I forget the minute I say them. I've never been this nervous on stage, so why here? The next thing I know, I'm saying, "What vision do you have for the future here, sir?"

"Education. Education. We need to learn the old ways and the new."

He winks at Susann. It's then that I notice, though it's been there all the time, of course, is that Uncle Albert is wearing an official-looking army veteran's cap.

"You were in the army, sir?"

"I was a sergeant in Korea. Big battles."

"My father was in Korea. Well, not actually in Korea. He was stationed in England but it was during the Korean War. Well, a few years after. I don't really know."

"You don't know? Well. What else don't you know? That was hard fighting in Korea."

While we are talking another man comes and sits down beside Susann. He is in his late sixties, impressive and thick-lipped, with a long gray ponytail. He looks very suspicious of who I am and what I want. He is staring, piercingly, never taking his eyes off me.

"Sir, I saw a soldier from Iraq dancing with his family."

"Good boy."

"There's been a strong history of Indian soldiers fighting bravely for this country. Why do it, sir, for a government that you say lies?"

"Either we fight . . . or Leavenworth."

The expression of the man who had joined us darkens and he crosses his arms. Susann rises and motions that I should be done. I say thank you to Uncle Albert. As we walk away I look back and see Albert Leclerc wheeling around to watch us as we go. The impressive ponytailed man places his hands on Albert's wheelchair. His expression looks anything but benign.

As I pull out of the grounds to begin our delayed long drive to South Dakota, Susann says matter-of-factly, "You know we've been testing you."

>>Dispatch: Adventure Is Never Planned
Sometime around 10:00 p.m. My Cell Is Out of Service

On the road to Vermillion, South Dakota, Susann and I talk about the kids, her life these last months since her husband left, the fact that she has a strong circle of family and relatives that protect them all. Susann tells me about the school she wants to build for her children. She's home-schooling so she can use traditional structures and language. She tells me she doesn't think she'll see it all come together in her lifetime.

"Remember the circle and the dancing?" She makes a circle on the dusty passenger window of the Aveo. "That is the sacred circle. It the only way to truly teach my people. The circle always has at the center a tree, the sacred tree. That is humanity, the individual, me, my children. The sky is above. The earth is below. With the four winds, the four directions—they meet all around us. If you are centered in this how can you ever be lost?"

I ask her how people outside the tradition can help. She answers, "Just get out of the way." I smile and she tells me she thinks I'm "smart for a white guy."

The road is empty and the night is black. My little Aveo headlights barely make a dent in the dark. There are no signs that even hint at Vermillion, South Dakota. I'm resigned to sleeping in the car. But then, just when the night is darkest, there it is like the proverbial dawn (if dawn were nine miles off the highway, just past the Super 8): Vermillion, South Dakota. Susann guides me to the Native Cultural Center.

She looks very tired. I am anxious to get on the road but don't want to leave her there alone. Indian time is going to get me sleeping in my car. I say I am willing to stay. Susann's eyelids are heavy but she tells me to go. Adventure is never planned and can only be had if you follow your instinct and say "yes" to things presented.

I said "no." I should have stayed. I should have witnessed the arrival of the twenty or so runners, some of whom had come from the Rosebud Reservation to support the youth of the tribes in a year that has seen suicides, a murder, and trouble. Some of the runners are from Red Lake, who'd experienced the terrible shooting there in 2005. I should have slept in my car and followed them down to Macy. I didn't. Instead I drove into the night. The whole ride I am dogged both by regret and by the lightning and thunder off to the west, and gaining.

Outside Onawa, Iowa, is an enormous white billboard on which is ominously written PREPARE TO MEET THY MAKER. That night it's backlit by flashes of lightning.

Outside Council Bluffs I see the carcass of a good-sized doe that had met her maker with the likely assistance of a truck or SUV. It dawns on me that if I get hit by a deer while in this black peanut with wheels I'll be a goner. I grip the steering wheel at 10 and 2 and keep my eyes peeled, glancing regularly at the brush and trees on the side of the road.

I distract myself with thoughts of what I can accomplish tomorrow. I'll work on the Standing Bear play.

What's the play's structure?

Ideas. I know I will make all this a one-man show. Yes. I'll call it "Standing Bare"! Crap, that sounds as if it would be a naked guy talking. I'm sure there's an audience for that. Not the audience I want.

Wait. "Standing Bare" might work. Yes, yes. I'm baring my—no, no. I've replaced a run for Native youth with this? Please, God, don't let a deer jump out and have "Standing Bare" be the last thought I have. Another deer carcass.

And there is the sign and the turn off into Nebraska City. That night I have nightmares of vampires with clutch purses, cowboy boots that walk on their own, and I'm a tourist in my own place of home. Could be test anxiety.

>>Dispatch: Documentaries
Wednesday, August 16. 8:00 a.m.

I have an appointment at 9:30 a.m. at Nebraska Educational Television (NET) to meet with Karen Fox. Karen is a nationally known and respected documentarian. She is also working on the Standing Bear story.

Karen is not what I expected. I expected, I don't know, a sort of academic Christiane Amanpour: editing with one hand, slapping her research assistant with the other, while screaming for more funding from the suits upstairs. Karen is unconventionally conventional. To give myself my due, she does looks a bit like Christiane Amanpour.

We sit down and jump right into the Standing Bear story. Did you know? . . . Amazing, isn't it? . . . and, Have you read? This is what happens when you get some folks talking about Standing Bear.

Wait. I realize that many don't know the story. Okay. So here it is, my documentary.

>>Dispatch: My Documentary

The Somewhat Brief, Highly Subjective, Somewhat Flip,
and Uncomplicated-by-Contradictory-Facts Version for You

The Ponca Tribe is part of the extended Siouan Language
Group/Omaha family of tribes. The Poncas were very small
in number by the time Lewis and Clark took note of them
while rowing up the Missouri with the Corps of Discovery. The tribe had come to what is now Nebraska from the
indeterminate east—neither scholars nor Native peoples
agree where from—at some point in the 1750s. Though
there is, of course, archeological evidence of people in the
area that goes back much, much farther. Much.

Unlike the Sioux or the Pawnees, who were sort of the
bedouins of the buffalo grass—but *like* their relatives, the
Omahas—the Poncas lived in permanent earth lodge settle-
ments. They were farmers who annually went on the buffalo hunts, like most tribes. This was during a time when
the Great Plains were a sort of Continental Commons—
used by all, owned by none. The area in which the Poncas
settled is, as I will always say, beautiful beyond words but,
more than that, excellent farmland with strategic views of
the Missouri River. Prime real estate.

Now, call up your high school American history and
remember that all the Indians were getting pushed out of
the East or dying off all over in the 1820s and 1830s. Last
of the Mohicans. Trail of Tears. It's all of a tragic Jackso-
nian piece. It was a heave-ho and a westward ho! for them
all. But, as you also no doubt remember—and likely have
heard a lot more about—white settlers were also heading
west and founding towns like Decatur, Nebraska—doing
dress rehearsals for Riverfront Days. Waxing lyrical, Jef-
ferson once predicted it would take a thousand years to

settle the West. It took only about sixty. The Poncas' numbers were further decreased by the smallpox epidemics of the 1830s. These epidemics completely took out the Mandans, who had been so good to Lewis and Clark.

After the Civil War and the question, "What do we do with the slaves?" the next big national cut-and-paste project was "What do we do with the Indians?" So, the Indian Wars. The Poncas were caught up in all the mess, right smack dab in the middle, territorially speaking. The Sioux, particularly the Brulée Sioux, bullied the Poncas mercilessly—burning farms, killing women and children—and, worse yet, accused them of living like white people. Meanwhile Nebraska was opened up to U.S. settlement in the 1850s. The Nebraska tribes were harassed on all sides.

So the red dirt of Oklahoma (Indian Territory, as it came to be known) is made the sunny destination for the Native peoples of Eastern and Middle America. A veritable "Who's Who" of once-sovereign nations was dumped where the wind comes sweeping down the plain. Begging the pardon of Rogers and Hammerstein, and of my relatives and friends from the Sooner State: it ain't all that and a bag of chips. Or at least it wasn't back then. Particularly if you were from an area Lewis and Clark described as Eden, Paradise on Earth.

The Otoe-Missouri tribes were the first from Nebraska to go. They'd been driven into Nebraska just a decade before, so they still had their bags packed. Then there were some pesky Cheyennes in the far west, but that was as easy as a few empty promises of payment and a regiment of cavalry. Next to go were the Pawnees—the bad boys of the plains. They went kicking and screaming a little, but they went. The Sioux, however, were a bigger deal. They were awesome to Lewis and Clark, but after the Civil War they became' an even more troubling force—too large to be packed off, too organized to be broken, and too pissed off to play nice. Witness Little Big Horn.

Then there were the Omahas. The Omahas epitomized the Jeffersonian ideal: genteel farmer-citizens industriously enjoying the bounty of the land and quietly living in democratic simplicity. Well, at least that's what their press kit said, because they were very smart and had insightful leadership who made good treaties and useful connections in Washington. They knew they were only buying time. But they understood, I guess, that Indian time can really mess with the European clock.

Finally, there were the unfortunate Poncas, living in paradise a little too close to the cranky Sioux. The Bureau of Indian Affairs, in the year after Little Big Horn, thought the Poncas had a swell stretch of land on the Niobrara River. In the BIA's wisdom they decided to give that land to the ornery Sioux—and let them think they were giving them something for all their bitching. The Poncas were few, they would have to accept it.

The Ponca chiefs (including Standing Bear) were shown their new home in Indian Territory. It was a guided tour worthy of a New York City realtor. "Riverview" meant "You can sort of see the river if you lean over this bluff while holding on to that branch." "Spacious" meant "the outhouse is in your earth lodge." "Landmark" meant "this land is so unusable you'll have to wait until the twentieth century, when they may discover oil on it, to be able to reap any benefit." The Ponca chiefs wanted none of it.

But what they didn't know was that they were already in escrow. The contract was signed and the Welcome Wagon was waiting in Oklahoma.

So, it's wintertime in Nebraska. That, by the way, is when the wind really comes sweeping down the plain. The Poncas set off on foot from the top of Nebraska, walked down the entire state, down the entirety of Kansas, and into what the Poncas call "the warm country" of Indian Territory. They are promised that the movers will be bringing their furniture and things later. Their possessions never arrive, and instead are sold off by the Indian agent only days after their departure.

Along the way a good number of them die, among them Chief Standing Bear's beloved and only daughter, Prairie Flower. She is buried by the good Christian women of Milford, Nebraska. The settlers along the way are so moved by the plight of these unwilling pilgrims that they give them food and alms.

The diminished and starved Poncas finally arrive in the "warm country" and promptly get sicker and sicker. Chief Standing Bear and his fellow chiefs complain and are whisked off to Washington for a pat on the back and a show—really, they were actually taken to a show. It was a musical, *Pink Pajamas*. I'm sure that made up for everything.

>>Dispatch: The Return Home
March 1878

Standing Bear's eldest son, Bear Shield, dies. He is sixteen or seventeen. With his last breaths the boy makes his father promise to lay his bones with those of his grandparents. Standing Bear promises. And, after his son's bones are dried, he places them in a leather sack. With about twenty or so other Poncas he walks all the way back up to Nebraska, making his way toward the Niobrara. A total of five hundred miles. Settlers along their way begin to get suspicious. I wonder if some who were so concerned about the Poncas' return were the same ones who had been so kind as they marched to their exile.

The group arrived at the Omaha Reservation, and the weary band was taken in by the generous Omahas. But, unbeknownst to them, Gen. George Crook—the Greatest Indian Fighter in the whole of the West and second-in-command under Gen. William Tecumseh Sherman—is charged with arresting Standing Bear and his posse for not staying put and not doing what the Great White Father told them to do. Arresting these people is something the eccentric, savvy, softy General Crook is loath to do. He thinks the wonks in Washington are a bunch of lily-livered, pasty-faced sheep guts without the sense the Good Lord gave a rock. Nothing changes. Crook is also a war buddy of Rutherford B. Hayes, the newly elected president of these United States. The general thinks he can make sure that Standing Bear will be freed, though some powerful wonks in Washington, such as the secretary of the interior and the head of the Indian Bureau, think otherwise.

Meanwhile, an idealistic but prone-to-exaggerating itinerant preacher and journalist named T. H. Tibbles gets word from an Omaha leader and his daughter of the poor Poncas and their plight. You see, they are now under arrest by order of the government and being held in the fort outside Omaha, and somehow it gets firmly planted in the heart and head of T. H. Tibbles that he will be the pen and the sword for these poor and wayward souls.

That Omaha daughter, by the way, is an Eastern-educated young woman named Bright Eyes "Susette" LaFlesche (half-Omaha, half-French) who dresses with Victorian precision at the insistence of her father. The father is powerful Chief Iron Eye. They live outside the Omaha Nation. The LaFlesche family is well known in these parts. They are called "the pretend white people" by other Omahas. Bright Eyes is the most beautiful girl in all the counties round. When Longfellow meets her later, he says that she is the embodiment of Minnehaha:

> In the Land of the Dacotahs
> Lives the Arrow-maker's daughter
> Minnehaha, Laughing Water,
> Handsomest of all the women.
> I will bring her to your wigwam,
> She shall run upon your errands,
> Be your starlight, moonlight, firelight,
> Be the sunlight of my people!"

With Chief Iron Eye and Bright Eyes pushing in the background, T. H. Tibbles gets even more fired up and speaks with his buddy, General Crook. Among the four of them they piece together an unprecedented and audacious scheme: Standing Bear will sue the American government for the right to go home.

General Crook is a brave soldier, a wise tactician, a reluctant mover through the corridors of power, and an infamous rattler of bureaucratic cages. Crook sets T. H. Tibbles to the task of getting the word out—nationally, if possible—and persuading some fine local lawyers to sign on. Crook, meanwhile, has to give every appearance of faithfully following orders from Washington, orders he in fact believes are inhumane and un-American. He enlists his devoted right-hand man, Lt. John Gregory Bourke, to help out. Loyal Bourke does so with sensitive enthusiasm and a touch of Boy Scoutishness. Lawyers John Lee Webster and Andrew J. Poppleton—two of the best in the area— are quickly engaged (pro bono).

At General Crook's own instigation, it is decided that Standing Bear should file a writ of *habeas corpus*—accusing General Crook himself (and, by implication, the U.S. Government) of wrongful imprisonment. According to the writ, Standing Bear has the right to appear before a court to answer charges and determine if, in fact, he has been rightfully imprisoned. All citizens of the United States are accorded this right. It's a safeguard against unlawful and arbitrary imprisonment, both in times of peace and in times of war. It was a radical plan, since no Indians had ever been afforded such rights—either as non-citizens of the United States living on "sovereign lands" or as a nineteenth-century subclass of the human species.

For three months T. H. Tibbles writes article after article heralding the news. He leaves his pregnant wife, Amelia, and by carriage and on horseback he tirelessly canvasses churches in Iowa, Nebraska, South Dakota, Kansas, and Missouri, appealing to the congregations to give aid and support. They unanimously agree, church by church, in the name of Love, Justice, and Jesus Christ. These days would many good Gospel-of-Prosperity Christians champion such a cause? Especially if they did not know—as many of the parishioners in those days did not know—that these "savages" were fellow Christians? Just asking.

>>Dispatch: Standing Bear vs. General Crook

April 30, 1879. Fort Omaha

The hearing (technically it was not a trial) begins, with Judge Elmer Dundy on the bench. General Crook, who by all accounts rarely wore a uniform, arrives in court in full dress military regalia: blue-black jacket, gold epaulets, red sash, medals, the works. The court is packed with mostly non-Native faces: churchmen, officers, and the curious of the surrounding towns and farms. Bright Eyes LaFlesche enters in demure Victorian simplicity, with a small ostrich feather–topped hat of the period. The courthouse itself is surrounded by the pitched tents of Indians (mostly Omahas). A few Indians are standing at the back of the courtroom.

Standing Bear's position, if he wins, will force him to give up all tribal affiliation. The lawyers suggest he wear a European suit to court. It will illustrate his desire to live in the civilized world of law and society. Standing Bear arrives in full Native regalia: his iconic bear claw necklace, U.S. government–issued two-treaty-earned silver medals around his neck (reminders to the court of promises made), a black-tipped eagle feather in his hair. He is wrapped in his personal blanket of honor and position. The blanket is respectfully draped just as his people drape their blankets when addressing a tribal council. Standing Bear speaks little English so an interpreter is provided; it's a young man who, according to an increasingly concerned Bright Eyes, is not very good at his job.

The federal district attorney argues that Standing Bear should have none of the protections of *habeas corpus* because he is not a U.S. citizen, nor is he—and here's the breathtaking part—even a "person" in the eyes of the law.

Standing Bear's lawyers in turn cite the newly adopted Fourteenth Amendment.

> Article 14, Section 1: No State shall make or enforce any law which shall abridge the privileges or immunities of citizens of the United States, nor shall any State deprive any person of life, liberty or property *without due process of law, nor deny to any person within its jurisdiction the equal protection of the laws* (italics are mine).

At first it's touch-and-go. One of Standing Bear's lawyers believes they've lost. The district attorney is sitting proud. But General Crook is smiling under his flaring red beard. Judge Dundy is ready to make his ruling. Standing Bear wants to speak. It is not certain the judge will agree that he should. It's not according to legal procedure in such a hearing. General Crook wants him to speak. Tibbles is ready to record it all and trumpet the news. But the hearing is technically over and there seems no need for the chief to speak. Everyone is waiting on Judge Dundy.

"Hear ye. Hear ye. Court is now adjourned." Judge Dundy directs the marshal to say this while facing the bench, in a barely audible whisper, in case Standing Bear understands more English than he lets on. He allows Standing Bear to speak for himself. He motions for Standing Bear to rise and address the court. Surprisingly, Bright Eyes steps up and motions to the young translator to step aside. She will translate. Bright Eyes is the same age and had been friends with Standing Bear's daughter, Prairie Flower, who died on the long march south. I wonder if Standing Bear thinks of Prairie Flower as Bright Eyes takes her place beside him.

Historians seem to agree that Standing Bear had not been prepared well. Tibbles, the storyteller, preacher, and writer, only told him what a good storyteller, preacher, and writer would advise: keep it short. The court, as courts and theaters do when something extraordinary happens, goes deeply, palpably silent. Truth is often reverenced by silence. Standing Bear holds out his hand. He doesn't say a word—just stands there with his empty hand extended in stillness, by most accounts more than a minute. The audience starts looking about and at each other. "Is this it? Is this what we've been waiting for? Oh, God bless the poor Indian!" Then Standing Bear finally speaks, Bright Eyes translating:

> I see a great many of you here. I think a great many of you are my friends. Where do you come from? From the water? From the woods? Or from where? God made me, just as he made all of you, and God put me here—on this land. But a man I did not know came and ordered me to leave my land. We walked south many miles. One hundred and fifty-eight of my people died in and on the way to that land in the south. I do not wish to die away from home. I want to go home, to live and be buried in the land of my fathers. I have hurt no white men. Once, out hunting, I found an American soldier on the prairie, almost frozen. We took him home, made him warm and fed him till he could return to his home. Another time, I found a white man who was lost and hungry. This man we also took home and fed and set him on the road to his own people. Had I been a savage, would I have not killed these men?

Then Standing Bear lifts up his hand again:

> [This] hand is not the color of yours. But if I pierce it, I will feel pain. If you pierce your hand you also will feel pain. The blood that will flow from mine will be the same color as yours. I am a man. The same God made us both.

It reminds me of something . . . "I am a Jew. Hath not a Jew eyes? Hath not a Jew hands, organs, dimensions, senses, affections, passions; fed with the same food, hurt with the same weapons, subject to the same diseases, heal'd by the same means, warm'd and cool'd by the same winter and summer, as a Christian is? If you prick us, do we not bleed?"—from *The Merchant of Venice* by William Shakespeare (ca. 1597). Standing Bear has no reason to have known this passage. Bright Eyes does. She is enamored of Shakespeare.

Standing Bear continues briefly to appeal to Judge Dundy for the freedom to go home. Standing Bear acknowledges that his fate is in the judge's hand. T. H. Tibbles reports that Judge Dundy had tears in his eyes, that General Crook covered his eyes and leaned on his hands, and that there was audible crying in the back of the room. Judge Dundy nods at the marshal. "All rise!" It's over. Cheers. Everyone crushes to get to Standing Bear. General Crook is the first to shake his hand.

They have to wait for the ruling, but it comes a little over a week later. Standing Bear is a "person" in the eyes of the law and has all the protections of that law!

The night the decision is rendered—thinking that immediately he has the freedom to do as he wishes—Standing Bear places the leather sack containing his son's remains and sets off on foot toward the Niobrara River and home. T. H. Tibbles and Bright Eyes become aware of this and leave after midnight to catch up with the still grieving father. They must stop him and tell him, as they've been warned by Crook, that if the Chief (now a citizen) sets foot on Indian land, he can and will be arrested. Washington wants this. The Dundy ruling has embarrassed and inconvenienced them, throwing into question their flawed Indian policy. At roughly the same moment that Tibbles and Bright Eyes take off on their midnight ride, soldiers have been sent without Crook's knowledge to intercept Standing Bear. Tibbles and Bright Eyes get there first and convince him to return to Omaha.

The case becomes famous in its day. Papers and magazines all over the world tell the tale of justice given. The participants became celebrities. Tibbles relishes his fame and the bully pulpit. He plans a tour of the East to gain support for the Poncas and the plight of the other Indian peoples. In Boston the poet Henry Wadsworth Longfellow becomes enamored of Bright Eyes. All of Boston is taken with her. A woman named Helen Hunt Jackson, daughter of a New England abolitionist, gets so electrified at hearing the trio lecture that she follows them to New York City and researches and later writes a classic condemnation of the treatment of the Indians, *A Century of Dishonor.*

When in Boston, Standing Bear and Tibbles are eating lunch in a hotel one afternoon and both receive telegrams. Back home, Tibbles's wife, Amelia, has died. Meanwhile, Standing Bear's brother, Big Snake, who had stayed in the Indian Territory, has been shot by orders of the head of the Ponca Agency. As the tour continues to Philadelphia, New York City, and Baltimore, Tibbles and "Bright Eyes" fall in love. They soon marry.

> She shall run upon your errands,
> Be your starlight, moonlight, firelight,
> Be the sunlight of my people!

Standing Bear finally goes home. He has a small house and quietly tends his garden and remaining family until he dies in 1908.

In 1962 the Poncas in Nebraska (the Northern Poncas) are abolished as an official tribal nation by an act of Congress. The eight hundred acres that were given to Standing Bear and those that returned with him are confiscated. But in 1990 the Ponca Restoration Act is signed into law by Bush the Elder. The Northern Poncas have their first pow-wow in 1993. My mother and I attend their tenth. That's when I get my first taste of this great American story.

Karen and I are passionately discussing this story in her office at NET. We speak for over three hours. We weren't on corporate time, we were on Standing Bear time. We discuss how few people around the country know the story.

>>DISPATCH: GO HOME
Lunchtime the Same Day. Madonna
Rehabilitation Hospital, Lincoln

Deb Steinkolk is still in the nursing home. The doctors do not know the nature of the MS or why it came on so quickly. Since I saw her last, Deb has had a brain scan and gained a little weight. Her parents, Alma and George, are there at the hospital every day. Her mother feeds her. Deb's father looks after her children.

Deb is speaking more. She says now, repeatedly, one phrase: "Go home." As I'm talking to Deb, her eldest son climbs onto the bed with her and she starts to cry. "I want to go home. Go home. Go home. Home."

Her mother strokes her hair and tells me, "She's having a bad day."

I stay for as long as I can, helpless to do anything but simply be there. I am thinking about home. Thinking about Deb's home, Standing Bear's home. I'm thinking about family. Thinking about my mother and father, my sister and brother, their families. How spread out we are. How my father brought us to Nebraska from wandering the Central Time Zone. How he and my mother made it our home. How my mother stayed here after my father died. She made it her home. How my sister and brother have made their homes, strong but different homes. I am thinking about my home and what that means to me. But I have an appointment at the State Capitol.

>>Dispatch: The Nebraska State Capitol
August 16, 2006. 3:00 p.m. The Wind Is Up

I have an appointment with Diane wawe'nohi. (The small "w" is intentional.) Diane is the executive director of the Nebraska Commission on Indian Affairs and the first member of the Ponca tribe I will meet on this visit.

The state capitol of Nebraska is a large, impressive art deco phallus on the plains. Often called the "Penis of the Prairie," the "Schlong of the Sage," the "Lincoln Log of Love," the "Wang of the West." It has a man sowing seeds to the wind on the top of the polished gold dome cap.

Stepping down into the lower lobby, the capitol building looks very much like the set for the Wicked Witch's castle in *The Wizard of Oz.* An exceptionally friendly receptionist inquires about my hopes and desires for my time in the capitol. She has brochures.

"Alright now, what neat person do you want to see here at the ol' capitol?" she asks.

"Diane wawe'nohi."

"Well, that's a funny name. *How* do you say it?"

"Way-wah-nah-hee."

"How does she spell it?"

I spell it.

"My. What does she do?"

"Department of Indian Affairs. I have an appointment."

"Sounds Indian-y. Shall I check the book?"

"Sure."

"Let me see. What did you think of the storms last night? Wow, right? Why, here she is! But look at this. They've gone and made a typo. Diane deserves a big old capitol 'W' like everyone else. I'll just take this pen and change it for her."

I watch her do it.

"Could you call her? I have an appointment. My name is Christopher Cartmill."

"I'll just do that. Are you going to talk about Indian Affairs?"

"Sure."

She holds up her finger to let me know she's got someone on the line.

"Hi there! Is this Diane? Hi! This is Andrea, downstairs. You have a visitor. Christopher Cartmann. That's great. Great. Okay. Bye, bye. Okay. Sixth floor. Just over there. Take some brochures!"

I head over to the small still-in-use 1920s elevators, all art deco woodwork. I look back at the reception desk, and Andrea grins and waves at me.

"Have a great visit with Ms. Diane "W.," Chris. And enjoy Nebraska! It's the good life!"

Diane is waiting for me as the elevator doors open. I know she has a daughter who is a successful lawyer in D.C., but Diane looks thirty. Jet-black bobbed hair and black nerdy glasses that not only don't detract from but even set off her beauty.

Above her desk is a large poster of the Standing Bear Trial (or, rather, hearing). The other walls are a mix of blankets, dream catchers, and event posters. Diane sits me down and presents me with a great quantity of pamphlets, brochures, and cards. She's smiling but she doesn't really ever look me in the eye—only intermittently and never for more than a glance. We talk about the Nebraska quarter design decision.

It was supposed to be Standing Bear—the only U.S. state quarter to have a Native theme. A big political statement. But the governor—hoping to garner votes in the even more conservative western part of the state—switched the coin to a depiction of Chimney Rock and a covered wagon. This has made Diane wawe'nohi angry. She wants everyone to know it. Interestingly enough, if the geographic orientation of Chimney Rock is right, the wagon is headed east! This must be comforting to Native peoples. Send 'em back.

Diane warms to me. She looks at me more often. She gives me more things, such as CDs, posters, and buttons. She says, with some finality, that I should and will meet the governor to tell him about the project, let him know that this story is "international in its relevance."

"Do you want to see the mural? The murals. Stephen Roberts painted them. Great artist. Lives in Omaha. He's got Standing Bear. You have to see it."

We go up in the tiny elevator all the way to the top sky-scraping gold dome. When we walk out I can feel the wind sweeping through the room. There are no windows up in the dome. It is partially open to the elements and this day the gusts of wind are so strong they toss my hair and shirt. We walk into the small marble rotunda up in the sky. The wind is whipping in and around us. Diane tells me she's hoping to have flags from each of the tribes that once lived in Nebraska installed here soon.

Six modern murals on canvases hang high on the six walls of the rotunda. The wind seems to bring your head up to look at them. One depicts soldiers from World War I to Iraq. They're to represent "The Ideal of International Law." Really? Firefighters and police to represent "Service." I get that. A soup kitchen serving homeless, for "Community." Good. Another one with uniformed military said to represent "Reconciliation and Peace." The women soldiers are holding little foreign-looking children. Okay. Doctors with a patient, for "Health." Got it. Then I look where Diane is standing, showing where the flags of the tribes will be.

There is Standing Bear holding his hand out. Bright Eyes is slightly behind and at his side. General Crook is seated in his uniform; townsfolk and Tibbles in the benches behind. Indians standing at the back.

The wind kicks up and knocks Diane and me almost off our feet. I look at the key to the meaning of the picture in the brochure Diane gave me. "Standing Bear Trial—The Ideal of Freedom."

"And all he wanted to do was go home," I think.

Just then—like a whip—the wind rips the brochure out of my hand and up into the air.

>>Dispatch: What Are My Intentions?
August 17, 2006. Nebraska City, Nebraska

It seems that things surrounding the Standing Bear story take on a grand and mythic scale.

I leave the Penis of the Prairie and drive the fifty miles to Nebraska City. I have an email waiting for me from Susann which says, in brief, that if I think I am being tested now, just wait. I am still considered a guest and soon the real testing will begin. Then, she writes, "folks will come in for the kill."

"What?"

I take a deep breath. I think, "Okay, a people who have endured generations of people taking are not so keen on outsiders who want something. But am I asking for something? Maybe I am, but what?"

Susann goes on to write that if I want something I've got to be willing to sacrifice for it. She asks me what I want. What are my intentions? (Yes, and what are *her* intentions?) Further, she tells me, I need to present her with—and be prepared to present others with—a traditional Native formal introduction: name, parents, grandparents, birthplace, and family. Am I, she asks, willing to go to the mat—if it comes to that—for what I want to know?

Wait. Stop. I just want to tell a story. Just a story! Okay? Whose story? Who owns this story? Does Susann? Do her people? They're not Poncas. Bright Eyes was an Omaha but back in her day they called her a pretend white person. Does the state of Nebraska own the story? Can it be bought? Am I expected to pay for it? And what's the price? I've been asking myself who am I in this, really? But now Susann's asking—and asking for a sacrifice.

"I am Christopher John Cartmill and I'm getting pretty uncomfortable with this." I knew in the early days here that I'd opened a can of cultural, artistic, and political whoop-ass on myself. But this is getting deep.

"My parents are Robert Samuel Cartmill of Wellington, Kansas, and Joyce Ellen Miller of Arkansas City, Kansas." Come on, it's only a play. Yes, it's a life. Not my life. But it's not theirs, either. Can I even tell this story without stealing someone else's story? Can anyone tell any story without stealing something from someone else's story?

"My grandparents were Roger and Eunice Cartmill and John and Lorene Miller, but John Peck and Gladys 'Mimi' Peck acted as grandparents." And, what's more, why have I become a stranger in what I wistfully, and now I guess wrongfully, thought was my home?

"I was born in Wellington, Kansas, thirty miles from the relocated Ponca Indian Tribe and Ponca City." Everyone around me is becoming a stranger to me. What's going on? I am a stranger. I am being told I am a guest here, a guest who'd better be prepared to be tested!

"My name is Christopher John Cartmill and I'm getting really ticked." This is my home! Don't test me! I'm not just smart "for a white guy." Don't tell me you'll go in for the kill! What does that mean, anyway? I didn't come here to play Cowboys-and-Indians. I don't care who took from you. I didn't take anything! It wasn't me! All I want to do is tell a story!

Most of these people don't even know who Standing Bear was, really! The facts. To you he's a dude on a coin that never got minted, a political statement. He's some politically correct historical Indian guy. No, he's a chief from another tribe you can make into whatever you want. How about a t-shirt? Maybe you're thinking of Luther Standing Bear, the Sioux leader, because you've got him on your stupid Web site claiming it's the other Chief Standing Bear. He got five horses shot out from under him? Right. To you he's just a good story!

"My story!" And now, Susann, who said she was my

friend, is telling me I'd better be prepared for more testing. I didn't come here for a moral and spiritual smudging! I will not be a stranger in the place where both my parents are buried! Wait. Susann never said she was my friend.

Along with that email, I also get one from a "tscoleri" that says simply,

> I hear tell we have four things in common. Meet me at the Mill at noon on Friday to discuss them.

Now it's getting noir.

>>Dispatch: Send—Reply
7:00 a.m. the Next Morning

I sit at a picnic table in a park along the Missouri River to contemplate the preceding questions and mysteries. The sun is low in the east. I watch a couple of fishing boats getting launched from trailers into the swift waters, headed south. Bees busy themselves as bees are wont to do. Butterflies the color of butter flutter and dart. Swifts and swallows pick off the smaller insects in low-flying aerial assaults. Woodpeckers peck wood, not stopping to ask themselves how much wood could a woodpecker peck. Nothing around me is questioned. Not the intentions of the butterflies. Not the rights of the bees to suck where they suck. It is just life lived. (Well, admittedly, not for the bugs getting eaten by the swallows and the swifts.) I stay watching by the river for hours, until something dawns on me.

I get the courage to email Susann. I go back to the apartment and sign onto my computer. I write to tell her how I feel like a stranger in my own place of home. "Don't make me a stranger."

Finally, I ask her if she ever felt that—being a stranger in her own home? "Is that the feeling your people have known?" Send.

Reply: "Yes."

>>DISPATCH: TSCOLERI

August 18, 2006

I leave for my noon appointment with the mysterious "tscoleri" a little later than I'd hoped. You see, I have to stop by the rental place to renew the temporary license plate taped to the rear window of my little rented Aveo. It is no little trip. I get stuck in the noon "rush minute" on 27th Street. It is amazing to me how quickly this town has grown.

I get to The Mill coffeehouse in the Haymarket District about twenty minutes late. The Mill is where Lincoln shows off its college town cred; where the liberal academic literati leech on the free wireless and mingle with the occasional pierced artist or hip hop/hippie, drifting dropout. My "tscoleri," who had said he would find me, is nowhere in sight. That is, if I could have known him by sight. He would find me, he told me. I may be too late. I buy a slice of quiche and sit down to wait to be found. It was quiche or a cookie as big as my head. The quiche seemed the better option, though now microwaved and in the full light of day it is a nasty slab of gray eggishness and globby grayer bacon. I'm only eating to look occupied. Another twenty minutes pass. The place is crowded. As I reach for a *Daily Shopper* abandoned on a seat at an empty table, a wiry, hard-bitten looking man in his early fifties strides up and towers above me. Immediately I observe that he personifies the gravitas of Clint Eastwood, the charming menace of Dennis Hopper, and a touch of Bogart cool. His voice is sandpaper and smoke. This is "tscoleri." Put him in a fedora then fade to black and white and I would indeed be experiencing a noir film. I'm Paul Henreid and I'm eating quiche.

"You must be Christopher," he gravels. "You do look like a younger William Hurt. Good for you. I'm Tom. Tom Scoleri. Our mutual friend, Karen Fox, told me all about you. Finish your quiche then meet me outside."

This last he says with a slight and intimidating spark of a grin. He leaves. I follow, dropping the quiche into the trash, which lands with an audible thud. I head out onto the expansive porch of The Mill. The porch looks down on the red brick streets and red brick buildings of the Haymarket.

Tom is tilting back in a chair, hands folded on his head and feet up on the brick half-wall of the porch. Beside him sits a tall thick-figured man smoking a majorly big cigar. Tom tilts forward and reaches over to pull over a dark green plastic chair for me. He sets it next to his chair facing out.

"Sit."

I sit. The three of us face the street in a breath of silence. Tom takes a sly glance at my cowboy boots. His reaction is neither approving nor disapproving. He's just taking note. I'm taking careful note of his face, which is deeply etched and weatherworn. The deep wrinkles run in patterns that don't seem to match the musculature of a face. One line begins up in his hair and runs down the side of his forehead, through the middle of his cheek, skirts his mouth, and ends at about the middle of his chin. He has an incomplete wrinkle of similar contour down half the other side.

"Karen told me about you. Did she tell you about me?"

"She told me you were finishing up a history of the Standing Bear case. She said you were concerned that we didn't step on each other's toes—the three of us. She told me you just finished."

"She told you right. Still got tweaking though. Bibliography, preface—that sort of thing. Hey, this over here is my friend, Robert Grady. We were just chewing it as we usually do."

This Robert takes the cigar out of his mouth and extends one of his large hands to shake mine. "Pleased to meet you."

"Robert is an artist over there in the Burkholder Project studios."

"I do portraits, mostly. Yep, I do."

"And damn good ones. Robert was also the first black police officer in Nebraska history."

"That I was, that I was." Robert takes a short drag and rubs his leg. "Just got my hip replaced. Doing better now. Can't sit for long. Came here in 1957 to play ball. Never left. This is what I get for the ball playing." He rubs his leg again and chomps on the cigar.

Turns out Robert Grady didn't just play ball. Robert Grady was an inductee into the Indiana Basketball Hall of Fame for his high school play alone. He was the first black player for Nebraska, in 1957, and twice named Midwest AAU Outstanding Athlete of the Year. Became the state's first black police officer. Made Nebraska his home. He is now a successful artist. As he said, he paints portraits, mostly, and is interested in family and ancestry. He's a good listener, and sits smoking and rubbing while Tom and I talk.

"Karen says you're a good sort. That you've caught the Standing Bear fever. I know it." Tom is a professor at the university, a professor of history. He has the Standing Bear fever and as we talk more about the story he gets agitated and passionate. He talks and looks further into the distance. I'm trying to discern what he's seeing by looking at him. Robert is looking over at us both, getting more and more interested.

"We need to be looking at this story as a nation. It begs all sorts of questions, doesn't it? Questions you don't even expect."

"I know," I say.

"Look here. We are giving up our freedoms daily and we don't even ask why. And giving them up in ways that we can't yet comprehend."

Robert blows a smoke ring and nods his head.

"We need to look at this as Americans. How did this one man, who didn't even speak English . . . how did this man bring out the best in everyone involved—Native and non-Native? Some (most of them, for God's sake) were never that good again. The man and situation tested them and even though they weren't perfect and, fuck, were as human and selfish as any one of us—when it was most needed they all acted with honor, generosity, and integrity. They knew what was right and they did it. What made that happen? There've been harder tests before."

Robert blows a billow of smoke and pulls the cigar out of his mouth. "Hold up. Stop right there. Now, I got to ask this: Do you think it's just some coincidence that three of you folks—a historian, the documentary gal, and a playwright—are working to tell this story? I don't think so. No coincidence to my way of thinking."

Robert lets this hang and then gets up and goes. Tom

leans back and says, "Christopher, we have to do this again. Where're you headed next?"

"The Ponca powwow up in Niobrara."

"Well, then, that's *five* things we've got in common."

He never told me the first four. I assume they are Standing Bear–related. The mystery continues.

>>Dispatch: The Ponca Powwow
August 19, 2006

It's raining most of the way up to Onawa. The sign doesn't actually say "Prepare to Meet Thy Maker." In point of fact it says, "Prepare to Meet Thy God." That's somehow more comforting, but why, I can't exactly say. And on the radio I've heard the same country song at least eight times on as many different stations.

> If you're going through Hell,
> Keep on going.
> . . .
> If you're scared don't show it
> You might get out
> 'Fore the devil even . . ."

Yankton is in the midst of Riverboat Days so the streets are filled with folks as I pass through. The bridge over to Nebraska is a solid one-laner. South Dakota–bound on top, Nebraska-bound on the bottom. The bridge arches steeply over the Missouri River, but I'm feeling confident since there's no grating and no chance a truck will come at me.

When I arrive on the Ponca Agency the powwow is underway but to call it in full swing would be a stretch. They must have started closer to the appointed time than Indian time. All in all it is a decidedly different affair from the

Omaha powwow in Macy last week. There are about twice as many spectators as dancers. The large dancing grounds are virtually empty. And here's the part that I remembered from last time: a great many of the dancers look like me.

A boy of about eight saunters past with a white blond mohawk and a grassdancer outfit, which in this case is a white polo shirt with multicolored ribbons sewn to the waist. There are little bold blonde girls who very well could be named Heather, Ashley, and Amanda. They are lined up on a bench wearing satin and Mylar fancy blanket costumes. These don't look like regalia. They look like costumes.

Who's the white guy here? Who really is the cultural tourist? Have we co-opted this culture so much that the lines are blurred? They're not blurred everywhere—clearly not in Macy. Are "Native" and "non-Native" more of a mindset and less of a racial and cultural designation? I'm not sure Susann would buy that. Or would she?

A steroidal blond man with Michael Bolton hair and a bone choker is selling dream catchers and "authentic Indian medicine bags" in a tent behind the emcee stand. And the emcee stand has a banner on it that says, "Sponsored by Wells Fargo Bank." The bank's logo has a covered wagon heading into a sunset. Wow.

At one point I recall that Diane wawe'nohi mentioned in passing something about showing someone the place where Standing Bear is buried. That'll be something I can do: visit his grave. That's authentic. Perhaps the wind will kick up again and I'll get the thrill of the mystery of it all. I can let go of the confusion.

I go to the grandstand right behind the emcee. A blonde girl comes up and she wants to know if I want a t-shirt. They are selling t-shirts that say "Standing Bear: Equality before the Law" for fifteen dollars. The artwork is the mural from the Nebraska State Capitol.

"I actually wanted to know if you know where Standing Bear is buried."

"Who?"

"Chief Standing Bear. Standing Bear. On the t-shirt."

"Oh. I don't know. Michael?"

A young man with the thick goatee comes over.

"Oh, they don't know where he's buried. People might come and rob his grave. Nobody knows. Want a t-shirt?"

"Okay."

"That'll be fifteen dollars. Sorry about the grave."

I am walking away with my wet t-shirt and I pass an older but indeterminately aged man. He's short and thick. He's got a well-worn and kind face. I think I remember him from four years ago. I remember my mother commenting on his unique dancing style. I stop him and introduce myself. He has shoulder-length black-but-turning-ash-gray hair. He has a thin braid down one side. His regalia is all fringe and worked-buff leather. He has a very broad eagle-feather fan and a leather shield of black, red, and white. He wears no head feather or horsehair bonnet. His moccasins are high and lined with dangling sheep's wool and bells. He has a pink bandana around his neck.

"My name is Orton Ridgeway. I'm a wild Indian."

I ask him about Standing Bear's grave.

"Oh, my friend, you'll never get a straight answer there. Oh, yes, and anyone who points you that direction and tells you it's this place or that, is likely sending you out to nothing. Oh, some elders know but they'll never let on. Some of them only pretend to know so's to sound important. Rest assured, he's in a natural place, natural prairie as he'd have known it. If folks knew where he was now, don't you think they'd go and build a monument on him? He wouldn't want to go through eternity with a monument on his head, would he? Would you?"

I thank him and ask if I can take his picture.

"I'm a ham. Go for it. You didn't tell me what you're doing here."

"I'm writing something. A play or something."

"About Standing Bear? Oh, I like that. Good for you."

>>DISPATCH: COMING ACROSS STARS
That Evening at Sunset

I leave pretty soon after my chat with Orton and head up to Yankton. The sun is coming down and it looks even more beautiful. I see those butterflies the color of butter, the meadowlarks and orioles, the swifts and swallows. Then I see what I have been dreading since my late-night ride from Vermillion: a deer. A deer is ahead, at the side of the road, its body ready to spring. She is looking down the road at me—directly at me. I'm not going that fast but I slow down. She doesn't move. She's staring at me, following my car with her head and eyes. I get alongside her. I know I should just slam on the brakes but I don't. She looks in the window of my passing rental. And then she starts running at full gallop through the grass beside the road. She runs beside my Aveo, keeping her eye fixed at me. We go side by side for roughly a hundred yards. She is a fawn just about to lose her spots. She keeps looking at me. I am ready to swerve if she makes a break for the road. At about a hundred yards she takes a hard right and darts back into the woods along and beyond the road.

Susann later tells me that a fawn's hide was used as a star map, a representation of the Pleiades. She says that they, the Omaha, believed they come from the stars. When I get back to Nebraska City I look up at all the stars. I can actually see the Milky Way.

>>DISPATCH: POCAHONTAS
The Next Afternoon. Nebraska City

I watch Disney's *Pocahontas*. When I go into Captain Video in Nebraska City to ask for it, you'd have thought I was asking for porn. A man with a maroon toupee who seems about seven feet tall leads me to the back of the store. It is not among the children's DVDs but in a category that actually is designated "Adult Drama." Maybe it *is* porn.

If you haven't watched the animated feature ever, or lately, it is a sordid trip. It is willfully historically inaccurate. I'm all for poetic license, and have used it, but this takes some stretching.

Why has this story been so much a part of the American psyche? It seems to me to be about the taking of the land (in the body of Pocahontas). The historical Pocahontas was ten or eleven years old, yet in two hundred years of versions she has been turned into a sweetly, savagely sexualized beauty who desires John Smith (or Colin Farrell) and is desired by him. Among a lot of things, I think, she is the beauty and fecundity of this land. She is the embodiment of our desire to possess it, to tame it, to put it in Western clothes and make it our home. It's just a cartoon, right? Susann tells me she will not watch it. Her children are not allowed to see it.

A Couple of Days Later

I take a field trip to the Lewis and Clark Interpretive Trail and Visitors' Center. There I am invited to:

> "Re-discover the adventure in a 12,000 square foot facility on 80 scenic acres."

On the outskirts of Nebraska City, high on a bluff overlooking and offering a spectacular view of the Missouri River, this is actually interesting, if not a little on the weird side.

> "Experience a unique and exciting perspective of the history-changing Corps of Discovery journey of Lewis & Clark from 1804 to 1806."

There is a replica of the Corps of Discovery's keelboat—from the IMAX movie of the expedition. Great parts of it are made of Styrofoam.

> "The center showcases over 300 scientific discoveries recorded by Lewis & Clark on their journey including flora and fauna specimens they sent to President Thomas Jefferson."

There are taxidermy specimens of everything from an elk to a grizzly bear. The bear growls at me as I pass it. Loudly.

> ". . . with hands-on exhibits testing your skill and challenging your senses . . ."

One display case has a mosquito the size of an average ten-year-old. The exhibit makes a raucous buzzing sound as I approach. I read that the mosquito was the bane of the Corps' travels. I am challenged to place my hand into a tube right under the mosquito's foot-long proboscis to see if I "can stand it." I did not attempt this.

"You can burrow with the prairie dogs & meet Pee Dee, the live prairie dog."

When I get to Pee Dee's lucite case, it is wide open and there is shredded newsprint on the floor. Pee Dee is nowhere to be seen.

The place is empty but for a woman at the desk and me. She is deep in a book. I am concerned. Am I going to be challenged to find Pee Dee? Will I be invited to place my hands in dark corners and under cabinets to see if I can stand it? I interrupt her reading and ask what happened to Pee Dee. I am blankly assured that Pee Dee is napping in the back. He gets easily stressed, the woman says. Stressed? By whom?

"Hike the Debruce Missouri River Overlook Trail and enjoy unobstructed views of the great Missouri River."

Beautiful, but mostly obstructed.

"Don't miss the most recent additions: the Plains Indian Earth Lodge and the birding exhibit."

This is what I came for: the earth lodge. It is enormous. I get a New Yorker's real estate envy. Buffalo hide rugs and bed covers. A bounty of food is placed on the table, all real and artfully arranged. Some of it is moldy and there is a large mousetrap under the table. The remains of a real fire cools at the center under the chimney hole. I could live here. But as I leave it strikes me that it was well-fixed with track lighting, which set off the appealing *Architectural Digest* look. This is not quite the authentic feeling I was going for, but close enough (for free). I don't follow the invitation to go birding.

>>DISPATCH: SUSANN'S HOME

August 24, 2006

When I get into Walthill that morning, on the way to Susann's, I bring a 310-piece art set and passel of Play-Doh for the kids. I also have a 310-piece set of concerns. One of which is: Is this the day that I cease to be a guest?

C. K.'s COWabunga Korner in Walthill, Nebraska. This is where I am to meet Susann. Walthill used to be non-Native but it is seeing a return of Indian families, which has created some tension with the non-Native Natives. Ironic, is it not?

I look out the window and see Susann's van. Martin is hanging out and waving at me. Susann tells me to follow them to her house, which I'm thinking is down one of the little streets of Walthill. It is not. We take off down Highway 77. We turn onto a dirt road bordered on either side by cornfields and sky. We drive for about a mile. Once over the crest of a hill, getting coated by the dust kicked up by Susann's van, the van turns into a gravel driveway.

Okay, here's where I want to be thoughtful and careful. I do not want to pretend I understand the universal, political, or personal forces that create and perpetuate poverty. Real poverty. Crushing, almost impossible poverty. Not the kind where you have to think twice about going out to eat with friends because the cable bill just came. No. The kind of poverty that shames all parties.

Just the facts, then.

First the facts: the 2000 U.S. Census states that the real per capita income of Indians living on reservations was less than half the average U.S. level. The real median household income of Indian families was half that of the U.S. median level. Though Indian unemployment was half the average U.S. level of 2000, Indian family poverty was three times the average U.S. rate. The share of Indian homes lacking complete plumbing was substantially higher than the U.S. overall level.

The house is tucked up against a small bluff on top of which is a field of corn in full tassel. A tall cottonwood tree behind the carport is being tossed around by the wind. Another van, broken down, is sitting in the carport. A broken sofa, a table, and two chairs are out on what is essentially the porch. Four children and two adults (before Susann's husband left) and three or four cats live in this house.

Martin runs over and takes my hand. Sophie comes up behind him, telling me how Valdis had predicted it would be windy that day. It is very windy. Very. I turn and look out over their view. The wind is in your clothes and hair. It is so beautiful—breathtaking and wide and I would have given anything to have played there when I was a kid— the fields of corn and soy waving through the uninterrupted hills. There's a small hefty gnarled-looking tree with a tire swing.

Susann opens the door and the kids rush in. I say I have a little something to give them. They jump up and down and the 310-piece art set and passel of Play-Doh are unwrapped and spread about the room before Susann has time to say thank you. She gets the kids to stop and shake my hand. Each does in turn. Martin hugs me. There are five rooms: bathroom, living-dining-kitchen, two bedrooms, office. Altogether only a little larger than my one-bedroom New York apartment. The four children sleep in one room. Sophie tells me that the cats sometimes pee there. Susann is in another room. The living-dining-kitchen is dominated by a large old sofa and a medium-sized kitchen table. A large television covers the front window. It's topped by a tank with a startlingly large turtle swimming in it.

Susann invites me into the office, which is her personal space, she says. It's the office of her school. It is where she has the computer and works with her children. The center floor tiles are gone. The desk and shelves are piled with paperwork and articles and books. The filing cabinet and broken closet doors are covered in free-form magic marker designs of green and black. Susann offers me a seat. She gives a deep, audible sigh. As we catch up, she takes out a handcrafted pottery bowl, a lighter, and some sweet grass and begins to smudge her face and the room with smoke. She doesn't explain it. She just does it.

We sit in the room for four hours discussing everything, from the Run for Indian Youth to her school, from my project to my family. Susann is adamant, no, passionate about Native teaching being the only way to give her children both a past and a future. She has sacrificed everything to make it happen. It has tested her. She tells me that many of her people don't understand what she's trying to do. I tell her, as the Bible says, prophets always get screwed in their own hometowns. But she wants her children educated to be fiercely Native adults.

Martin brings in the Play-Doh and makes a Doh handlebar moustache for me. I put it on and start talking like Yosemite Sam—an unrecognized irony. Martin tells me that they have a father but he had to go away. Susann shows me their wedding picture. Little Jewel stares at it. Susann pulls out a small family album of the kids. Each baby picture is so easy to name. Sophie, born elder. Valdis, concern. Martin, sun breaking through clouds. Jewel, wise mischief.

I feel out of all elements. I see an ominous red paperback on the shelf next to me with the title, "For Indigenous Eyes Only." Susann tells me it's about decolonization. She assures me it's about changing a mindset. I'm pretty certain it's a plan for sending me back to Europe.

Valdis asks me if I want to see their tire swing. Susann says that I should go and she'll call down to Macy—we'll be going to see her aunt and some of the elders today.

The sky, the field, everything is so beautiful. Valdis says that their father made the swing. Martin tells me the broken van is their father's. Martin leads us into the cornfield. They show me where they play and where their cats live and frequently give birth. We each pick an ear of corn. Valdis offhandedly tells me that that is all they have to eat sometimes. Then I realize I haven't seen the kids eat since we met up with them at 11:00 this morning. It's now almost four in the afternoon. The kids and I run down the steep part of the bluff. The wind kicks up and presses down the soy in waves.

Susann is seated outside. I tell her how beautiful it is. She tells me that she'd like to have known what it looked like before settlement, before her people and my people were there. "I would like that too," I say into the wind.

The phone rings. Her aunt is in the office. Like a shot, Susann runs into the house for the keys and tells the kids to get ready. They want to take the Play-Doh with them. So it takes longer than hoped. The boys want to ride with me.

The Tribal Council is a large building in Macy, Nebraska. The interior is configured like an enormous earth lodge. The minute we get inside, the kids go quiet. And I get ushered into a conference room where Marguerite Baker is standing. She has none of the welcoming energy she had during the powwow. In fact, she looks noticeably put out. She is put out with lots of things, including me.

>>DISPATCH: DANCES WITH WOLVES
Immediately Following

"I've been at a meeting with the Iowa Gaming Commission all afternoon," Marguerite says. She tells me that most tribes are not getting rich by these casinos. They're helping a little but not a lot. Tribes like the Omaha are getting, in fact, very little: a few jobs, perhaps, but the major profits are going to managing organizations—non-Omaha, non-Native, not even local. Marguerite is trying to cut a better deal. She is having a bad day; not only because of an Iowa Gaming Commission meeting, but a dear friend and fellow elder has died and she is late for the first day of the four-day funeral rite. On top of all that she has to meet with a playwright from New York City, whom she now knows is not a filmmaker. This disappoints. "Well, can we start?" she sighs.

I ask about Standing Bear.

"I can't really help you. You need to talk to the Ponca about Standing Bear. We don't speak for each other. You'll have to get their elders' permission to use the language. You know that. You'll have to speak before their council."

This is news to me. No one said anything to me about this.

"And you'll need to gift each elder you speak to. You should think of about one hundred dollars an elder. It's the way. It shows respect. That way, they won't think you're stealing from them."

This is also news to me. A hundred bucks a pop?

"Ideas have value," she says. "Stories have value. These people have value. You must understand that. One hundred dollars is small. You know *Dances with Wolves*? The Sioux went to Kevin Costner recently and asked for money to set up a tribal school, like Susann is attempting to do. He made, what? Three hundred million from that movie? He tells them no. What do you make of that?"

I'm not sure what I make of it, really, other than that I'm not sure whether I must pay Marguerite after we're done talking or if I can even afford to write this play. "I'm so tired. I didn't sleep all that well last night. Oh, my. I just negotiated for a new Propane Distribution Center. Do you know how much we were paying? But it will be ours now, no middleman. We've made progress but there's so much more."

Later I look through "*American Indians on Reservations: A Databook of Socioeconomic Change between 1990 and 2000 Censuses*," written in 2005. In it Jonathan B. Taylor and Joseph P. Kalt have written, "the gains in Indian Country could easily be reversed. Such a reversal would dash prospects for socioeconomic progress in Indian Country and would increase demands that federal and state governments address the problems of reservation poverty. That would be a losing proposition for all." They go on to explain that the gains are heartening but small. They cite other statistics like the "percent of persons under sixty-five without health insurance: 35 percent."

I go to the CDC Web site and find this:

Recent statistics show Native Americans 2.6 times more likely to have diabetes mellitus as non-Hispanic whites of similar age. Other causes of greater than average mortality include tuberculosis, suicide, pneumonia, influenza, and homicide. Finally, deaths attributable to alcoholism are also alarmingly high among American Indians.

These are statistics of which Marguerite Baker is well aware. Marguerite brings up the bad year: four youth suicides and two murders on the Omaha Reservation. "I don't want Red Lake here."

"Red Lake?"

"March of 2005. At the high school on the Red Lake Indian Reservation in Minnesota, a teenager went on a shooting spree and killed nine people before turning the gun on himself." I look it up. March 21, 2005. This is what Dr. Yvette Roubideaux writes in an article entitled "Beyond Red Lake":

> Most of the news reports highlighted his past, including a history of depression and suicide attempts, and the daunting socioeconomic conditions in his reservation community. Reporters mentioned high rates of poverty, alcoholism, unemployment, and violence among young people as possible factors in the tragedy. Although similar events have occurred in wealthier communities—the shootings at Columbine High School in Littleton, Colorado, leap to mind—this calamity seems to have reminded our country that many American Indian and Alaska Native communities face deep-rooted challenges every day and continue to be affected by significant socioeconomic and health disparities.

"We can't afford more losses," continues Marguerite Baker. I moved back home fourteen years ago. I've taken on leadership I wasn't supposed to have. I won't see that happen here."

"You moved home?"

"Yes. I was raised in Lincoln. Didn't Susann tell me you were too?"

"Sort of."

"When I got here I didn't like it. I wanted to go home. I could be working at an office in Lincoln and making . . . But it was important to come home. There's so much to do. Money, education . . . and the poverty. You've seen it. Take Susann, here. She won't tell you but I'll bet she doesn't have a dollar in her pocket. All of it goes to her kids and the school idea. That's all. I've got to go. Best of luck."

In the parking lot I tell Susann that I'm hungry and ask if I could take the family to COWabunga Korner for dinner. All the kids but Jewel ride with me. Valdis is concerned that the COWabunga Korner will close before we get there. Martin rolls down the window and we head back to Walthill.

Dinner is full of laughter, and Martin and Valdis sit on either side of me. Sophie keeps Jewel from bouncing in her chair. I feel like their father. I envy him the joy he has made. I pity him the loss of that joy. The food arrives and we feast on chicken tenders, curly fries, COWabunga burgers, cheese balls, and Pepsi—nothing green for miles.

Susann is doing a sweat lodge tonight (in honor of her run) so we have to be back in Macy at 8:30 p.m. I'd mentioned that if Susann needed some help with the kids during the sweat lodge I'd be happy to help. I was in a mood to see this through and live the "yes." As we're packing up I mention the gifting to Susann. She says it's The Way. Then she looks uncomfortable and asks, "If I could have money for gas, that would be helpful."

I pull out a twenty. That leaves me with two dollars. But

it dawns on me with little grace that I have a credit card and a bank account. I'm struggling in my own way but I can afford gas. I stand by the van while Susann goes to pay. The kids have heard nothing of our exchange and then Martin steps over Jewel and Valdis and comes to the van door and opens it. "You know what, Christopher? I love you." Without thinking I find myself saying, and meaning, "I love you, too, Martin."

>>Dispatch: A Sweat Lodge
8:30 p.m. The Four Hills of Life Wellness Center,
Macy, Nebraska

This is an addiction treatment center. The sign over the door says, in both Umonhon and English, "A New Way of Life." Susann is attending this sweat lodge to focus energy from the run and all she's been through these last months.

I see a man carrying a drum. Susann and the other women come out in long muumuu-like dresses. I am completely ignorant of the sweat lodge ritual.

Everyone has towels, so I think I get the sweating part. Susann tells me that she'll be getting answers and challenges. That is the extent of my understanding because I spend almost three hours watching NickToons and playing dominoes, hangman, and tic-tac-toe with Valdis, Sophie, and Martin. Jewel is completely self-sufficient and cares only for SpongeBob.

At about 11:30 p.m. folks start filing in and looking very tired. It looks like big things have happened. I know they were happening inside me. My SpongeBob sweat lodge. In silence we go to our cars. I shake Susann's hand and depart. I choose the wrong direction and proceed to get terribly lost. Literally Lost in the Night. Just me and the Aveo. A three-hour drive turns to five.

>>DISPATCH: MISSED
The Next Day

I receive an email from Susann saying that Martin did not know that I wasn't coming home with them and cried into the night. I try calling him. Neither Susann's cell nor office phones are in service.

>>DISPATCH: RIPPLES
August 27, 2006

I learn that there are over 4 million residents of the United States who can claim American Indian or Alaska Native ancestry, in whole or in part. I am not one of them. I also learn that two descendants of L. Frank Baum, the writer of the Oz books, publicly apologized for an article their famous great-great-grandfather wrote calling for the extermination of the Indians. Before he created the Wonderful World of Oz, Baum was an editor of a South Dakota paper. "Having wronged them for centuries," Baum wrote in 1890, "we had better, in order to protect our civilization, follow it up by one more wrong and wipe the untamed and untamable creatures from the face of the earth." Within days of the appearance of these words some 150 men, women, and children were killed at the nearby town of Wounded Knee. Among the survivors were the ancestors of the Cloud Horse children. Are we living in the ripples of events of so long ago? Or are we the ripples?

Why should we care about the events of 1879? And are our choices now a part of what was then? Are we now in a place we call home? Are we? Are you? And what is home, anyway? An inheritance? A destiny? A right? A choice?

In Disney's porn *Pocahontas* an ancient willow with the voice of Linda Hunt explains that the ripples from a stone dropped in the water grow larger as they move further from the place the stone was dropped. Yes, Disney, they grow larger, but what she doesn't say is they also grow broader, flatter, and weaker. A new stone needs to get dropped to stir the water up again if movement is wanted. Is that new stone an apology? A play? A meeting? A documentary? A connection? A drive up the highway? A friendship? A dispatch?

I keep asking who I am in this story. Who am I to add to what Standing Bear said or did not say so eloquently with his hand extended in a minute's silence?

>>DISPATCH: LET THAT BURN INTO YOUR MIND
Two Days Later

I drive back up to Walthill for a couple of hours to say good-bye to the Cloud Horses, particularly Martin. As I follow Susann's van into a parking lot, Martin sits in the back window waving at me. When the door opens, he tumbles out and runs across that lot then jumps onto me in a big, weather-changing hug. He wants his father. I am not his father. How am I a part of his story? And how is this a part of the story of Standing Bear?

Is it part of the story that while I am back in Lincoln I go into a Mexican grocery and see a sign that says, in English, "Support Immigration," and, in Spanish, "This Is Our Home, Too." Or is it part of the story of Deb Steinkolk being told she gets to go home? Though she and her family know that home will never again be the home it was?

I get another email from Susann. She writes,

> "I hope that with what you are learning about Native people, you will see that by telling this story about Standing Bear, you will gain a greater understanding which will also bring a greater understanding to the mainstream culture. But, you must also know the price. Anything you do will require a sacrifice, just like what I have paid. Yet, it will make you a stronger, better human being. Let that burn into your mind."

I hear my father's voice as I write. I feel my mother's joy. My mother in particular seems there for all of this.

>>Dispatch: Turbulence
May 6, 2007

There are only seven people on the 7:00 a.m. flight from Newark to Omaha. I haven't planned my trip well—I have a whirlwind week of meetings, events, and a performance, all surrounding the Standing Bear anniversary and celebration.

As we are taxiing to take off, I notice a lone woman sitting across the aisle. She is grinning and red-faced. I'm also aware that she has been staring at me for some time. When I glance up she says, "Are you famous?"

I say "No," grin, and get red-faced too.

Then she says to me, "Oh, if you aren't, you should be, by the looks of you."

If she's from Nebraska we may have crossed paths. There is such a thing as "Nebraska famous." The woman is chatty. She tells me she has been visiting a friend in New York, doing a lot of casual drinking and power shopping. She is heading home to Lincoln from Omaha, too, and wants to know if I would care to join her in the van that links Omaha to Lincoln. Before I can really answer, the woman is on her cell and talking to someone named Sean. Sean would be happy to take me as well. Sean will be waiting. Sean sounds nice.

I hadn't planned my arrival very well, so here was a plan. The woman tells me that she believes there are no "accidents." Out of the corner of my eye I see her take what I assume is some sort of sedative, which she downs with a glass of six-dollar airplane champagne. She slips into a deep sleep. She likely knows that we are going to pitch and bounce our way over the storms pounding the middle of the country. We do. To distract myself I read over my notes and research for the play I am going to write.

>>Dispatch: Landing and Coincidences
Omaha's Eppley Airfield

We make our descent into Omaha through a gap in-between strong storms. From the air I can see the Missouri River spilling out and over into fields, farms, roads, and towns. Anything that isn't under water is a rich Irish green color or the saturated black-brown of tilled earth. Paradise. Strangely, as we lurch toward the gate the flight attendant welcomes us to "Oklahoma." Not just once but twice. "Enjoy your stay in Oklahoma."

Omaha to Lincoln is a roughly sixty-mile trip. The woman from the plane just happens to be in the van with me. She asks my name again. "Wait. Oh, yes. Did I know your mother? Yes, I did! She was married to Dr. Withers. Oh, yes, I met her." The woman's face changes. "You must have mixed feelings about your father."

"He isn't my father."

"Oh, that's right. Your stepfather. You must have mixed feelings about him," she repeats.

"Not mixed," I answer with as little inflection as I can muster.

The woman smiles, lips pressed together tightly, and gazes out onto the highway. I look off to the heavy gray clouds scrumming on the horizon.

"I'm sorry. I—I hope you don't mind me saying this, but I went to his wedding reception. It was a business thing. Oh, but so quick after your mother . . . And now, as I understand it, they are living in your parents' house and sitting on your parents' furniture."

"It's not quite like that. Don't worry about us."

"Is it hard not to be able to go home?"

"It's not important. It's not my home anymore."

>>Dispatch: Pride and Shame

May 10, 2007

A rehearsal is scheduled at the Center for Great Plains Studies in Lincoln. I am performing a solo work, *The Dispatches*, based on my first Standing Bear summer. When I walk into the center I see the center's director and curator, Sayer Howard—whom I had met just after my mother died. Four years ago Sayer had shown me a collection of Tidball photographs from the Nebraska Native powwows. It was then that the Standing Bear story was starting to take root in my heart. Sayer is setting up for another exhibition and this will be a backdrop for my performance.

The wall before which I am to perform is lined with

paintings of homesteaders. On the right is a bronze table-top statue of an ox-drawn covered wagon; on the left, another bronze of a stagecoach frozen in a mad dash. The irony is not lost on me or Sayer.

I run through bits and pieces of my first summer's story of history and homeland. Sayer, whom I'd thought hadn't been listening, says, "It's the pride and the shame."

"Sorry?"

"The pride and the shame. You've got it, too. Your great-great-grandmother was Native, wasn't she?"

"Yes."

"All of us, with even a little blood in us, know it. Howard is an English name."

"So's Cartmill."

"Yes. Let me show you something," he says, and goes off into his office. He places in front of me a long folded sheet of paper. It's a family tree. He points down to one of the names.

"It's the pride and the shame."

The name I see first is Rolfe. And then I look to where Sayer is pointing. Rebecca Rolfe, Pocahontas. Sayer Howard is a direct descendant of Pocahontas. He smiles at me and says, "We feel the pride and the shame."

I don't tell him that I don't even know the name of my great-great-grandmother and that there is some debate in my family about which tribe she was a member of. That's shame.

I walk out of the center and look up at the sun. I drive down to St. Matthew's Episcopal Church. It is a beautiful little church that my father always thought looked like it was plopped there from the English countryside. I walk into the columbarium. There is a brass plate that says,

Joyce Ellen Cartmill
Robert Samuel Cartmill

I touch the plate, not remembering that this very day is the anniversary of their marriage.

>>DISPATCH: ANNIVERSARY BREAKFAST
May 11, 2007. The Embassy Suites in Downtown Lincoln

A large banquet hall is filled with people gathered to commemorate the anniversary of the Standing Bear Trial and celebrate the Native peoples of Nebraska. There is a long table on a dais at the center of which is a podium; the dais also holds seats for the chairman of each of the remaining tribes of Nebraska: the Santee Sioux, the Omahas, the Winnebagos, and the Northern Poncas (descendents of those who returned from Oklahoma with Standing Bear, and one of whom is Diane wawe'nohi). Fifty or so large round tables are scattered throughout the hall.

I find Diane and introduce her to Marie Green, the director of my solo show, who has come from New York City to work with me. I see Diane's daughters. They are as beautiful as their mother—sleek black swans moving in tandem through the room, attentive and self-aware of their own presence.

We find our table in front of the dais, on the side with all the tribal chairmen. Arriving at the table after us is an extraordinarily tall man with a ponytail. Bill Tall Elk is Sioux. He is an artist. He appears to list a little to one side, not from some malady but from habit and simple inclination. It's the way he needs to look at things, perhaps. His eyes are deep and gentle. He is accompanied by an elegant non-Native woman with light gray hair in a darker gray flowing dress. In all the clinking and talking I try to catch her name. She is Kate. She is Bill Tall Elk's wife.

Diane comes to the podium and welcomes the assembled. She dedicates this Standing Bear commemoration to the women of the Native communities. She mentions that abuse of women is a large problem. There is nodding from the tables all around. Interestingly enough, though, the tribal chairmen on the dais right in front of us look disinterested, even bored. I catch a glimpse of a figure next to Diane who is almost completely lacking in presence. I realize he is the governor of Nebraska, Dave Heinemann.

The chairman of the Sioux begins with an invocation. It has the rambling, free-form quality of an emcee's patter at a powwow. Diane motions to the governor. What he says leaves no impression whatsoever other than it seems to have been written with very little thought and is presented in such a way that shows even less. At one point he calls for the next day to be here and henceforth designated Standing Bear Day. After his duty is done and with precious little charm he steps off the dais and out the door.

Between speeches Bill Tall Elk and his wife ask me about what I am doing. I give the brief. Bill asks me my name again. We all politely turn our attention back to the speakers. At the end of the keynote Bill hands Marie and me each a small paper torn from a notebook. Each has a pen drawing with our name incorporated into the drawing. Mine has three horses in full gallop with "Christopher" written on the cheek of one. Marie's has a single horse in motion.

>>DISPATCH: BREAKDOWN
Noon. The Standing Bear Celebration

It's time to walk down to the capitol for the noontime Commemoration Celebration. We arrive in the Rotunda just as the honor guard is presenting the colors. This is a Native honor guard. An Omaha elder gives the prayer, in Umonhon. Opening remarks and introductions.

A musical selection by the Little Cook Family Drum. Then a piece by the Omaha Nation Junior-Senior High School Concert Band, an Indian tune begun by a Native flute then followed by the orchestra joining in to explore the melody. It is raw, lovingly rehearsed, powerfully sincere, and so, so beautiful.

Next we get to hear the governor's proclamation—declaring this to be "Standing Bear Day." The governor does not declare it himself. The lieutenant governor does. He doesn't seem to understand the dynamics of the microphone and makes just about everyone's ears bleed.

Next are presented the Essay Contest winners from middle and high schools in the state. Only one winner is in attendance—a gangly white teenager in shorts and a ball cap. He takes his plaque and gives the peace sign. His essay compares Standing Bear to Martin Luther King Jr.

The next thing that happens is, well, something like watching a car crash in all its blurred and vivid detail—a searing, subjective slow motion. Only I'm not observing. I'm in the crash.

An area high school is awarded for a successful production of an adaptation of *Black Elk Speaks*. The introduction of the award made it for all the world sound like they had created the adaptation, which I knew they had not. There is a slight dramatic pause, then a man in his late thirties with something of my coloring and my height rises to the podium. He takes a breath of mounting drama and launches into a loud Sioux invocation of the Four Directions. Something like:

Yuta-Heye! (*shaking joined hands to the East*)
Yuta-Heye! (to the *South*)
Yuta-Heye! (to the *West*)
Yuta . . .

I feel the blood rush out of my head.

He then speaks of all that he and his students have done to bring to life the spirits of Black Elk and his people—how he had done much honor to his brother, Black Elk. I feel the air in the room shifting, but no one else seems to react. A whirring sound starts in my head. A crash, a storm, thunder. He wraps himself tightly in a presentation blanket and speaks again. But what are we doing? Taking a story and making it your own. And what am I doing writing a play about Standing Bear? This is his day and I'm intruding. That's not writing. That's conquest. I don't have the honor of calling him my brother. I don't even know my great-great-grandmother's tribe or even her name! And can I wrap myself in a blanket of a story that isn't mine—a home I haven't really lost? I can't get the blood back into my head.

A woman is speaking, but I only hear bits in and among the thunder in my head. "I've learned of how sad it is, what these people have been through." I look at my cell. 12:30 p.m. Marie looks at me carefully and asks if I want to leave.

"I don't know," I say, "you decide."

"Okay, we're leaving."

I remember turning to those next to me and saying something about having an errand to run. Marie pulls me out into a corridor. I get halfway down the hall and burst into tears. Uncontrolled sobbing. I look up and through my tears I see the bust of Bright Eyes LaFlesche. This starts me sobbing again. A grown man weeping in the state capitol— probably not as rare an occurrence as one might think. The corridor is a dead end, so Marie and I have to double-back into the crowded Rotunda to go out the other side— down into the depths of the building. I lean against a marble wall. Marie has been quietly leading and following the storm in my face. After a bit she softly and simply asks, "Are you afraid that's you?"

"Yes."

>>Dispatch: We Have to Change That
May 11, 2006. The Center for Great Plains Studies

At the reception after my performance a friend of my mother's says, "Your mother would be proud."

The reception divides quickly and all too easily into Native and non-Native sides. As the evening draws down, a high school friend mentions that she would like to meet Susann Cloud Horse, who'd read one of her poems after my performance. "How I admire you," my friend says to Susann. "I've lived in Nebraska all my life and I didn't know the story Chris told. I didn't know this world even existed. That's a shame."

Susann smiles and then looks at me with a look that says, "Didn't I tell you?" But my friend reaches out to touch Susann's arm and says, "We have to change that."

>>Dispatch: Healing

May 12, 2007. Macy, Nebraska

My last day in Nebraska after the performance of *The Dispatches* is spent in Macy. Susann and her mother have invited me to the graduation of one of Susann's nephews, Harlen. Harlen has been raised solely by his grandmother, Elise Leclerc, and this graduation was a big deal. Marie and I both drive up for the event. This is after a great deal of back and forth about even going—the emotional and physical exhaustion of the week has settled into our bones. We arrive just as the twenty or so graduating seniors are being marched into the Macy High School gym. They are marching into chaos—a deafening chatter and perpetual motion. The bleachers are a beehive of relatives. A good portion of the audience is children. The immediate families of the graduates are seated on the floor. The faculty sits up on a disconcertingly high platform that the graduates have to ascend. Susann is seated with her children in the center of the bleachers. Martin runs over to me, shouting at full voice, "Christopher! Christopher! Christopher!"

Sophie Cloud Horse motions for us to come sit with her. She hands me a notebook and beams.

"THE MACY DispatchES by Sophie Cloud Horse.

Dispatch: Lincoln, NE. 6:00am.

VALDIS How ARE SAILS (?)! Says MY COUSIN HANDING US two Dollars for two pepsis! i SAY GOOD! HOW aBOUT you? SHE says good! WHEN SHE goes we see uncle Tony coming HE SAYS Hello and HANDS us A Dollar for a Bottle of WATER. SO that MAKES three Dollars So i Get out and [these guys 12 Rocks (?)] ME A FLUTE! WHEN i'M

GOING Back i see Martin Run by! So i CHASE after hiM AND WE BUMP into MOM AND A MAN AND HIS NAME WAS christopher!

DISPATCH: MACY POW WOW!

"Martin get back here! Come on Valdis! Okay! Martin! Oh HELLO. Chris Grandma and Mom are COMING!"
    Okay! He says.
    THE END!"

This is Sophie's record of our first and second meetings. I am moved.

The graduation bangs and rattles on. Sitting in front of us on the bleachers is a man I have seen before. He came to the performance the night before. He is a big, bearded, gruff man with soft eyes. Sam. Sam, it turns out, was adopted by the Leclerc family. He cares a great deal for Susann's family. A great deal. That day he is particularly solicitous of Elise Leclerc, who is standing off to the side of the gym, holding a blanket for a gift.

Sam turns back to introduce himself. We talk. At least I think we talk. I can barely hear anything. I confess that I catch only bits and pieces of the conversation. Martin is driving a Hot Wheels car—a car he calls "Chris"—back and forth over my head. Jewel keeps popping up from below, between my feet. "It's hard to come back," Sam says. "But the people here are so beautiful . . . but so pitiful."

Sam tells us about his tour of duty in Vietnam. How in his first week over there in heavy fighting he came upon the body of a friend who was cradling a Vietnamese infant in his dead arms. Sam says at that moment he'd stopped believing that anything he knew was right. "Everything changed. Everything."

Sam took up a study of Taoism and later investigated the belief systems of the Native cultures. He met the Leclercs sometime in the eighties and a decade later was adopted into the family by Frank Leclerc, one of Susann's uncles. Sam tells me about the spiritual gifts and long tradition of "heavy medicine" held by Susann and the Cloud Horse family. This, Sam believes, is especially true of Susann's children, who possess a convergence of spiritual energy they received from both parents. "It makes them especially at risk. When you're that sensitive to the force of God, or The Way, you can so easily slip into despair, addiction, or loss. Those tuned to a higher frequency always have a hard time of it, unless they keep tuned in. And even that's hard."

The graduation ends. We head up to a room in the high school that's been reserved for the Leclercs. It looks to be the cafeteria. A big feast is spread out across the room. There is a twin-sized mattress of potato salad, six regiments of hot dogs all neatly in line if not at attention, hamburger patties that could easily be remolded into the entire original cow, bags of chips that are as big as toddlers. When all is ready and all are assembled, one of the elders says a blessing and congratulates the graduates and then invites the honored guests to start the feast.

Sam pulls me aside when the cake is brought out. The cake, by the way, is the size of a queen mattress. "I don't think you know," Sam says, turning his soft eyes away, "what a healing you've done for this family. I can't tell you."

"Really? How?"

"That's all I'm going to say. Those children. It's a healing."

"I don't know about that, but I've gotten my own."

"You don't know how much has changed."

>>DISPATCH: CHANGES
August 5, 2007

"So here're your keys. The shift to reverse is a little sticky," declares my friend at the Lied, who is generously lending me a car to use during my stay for my second Standing Bear Summer.

"I'm sorry?"

"It sticks. Reverse. You look puzzled."

"It's—a—stick . . . shift?"

"Yes. Didn't they tell you? You have driven one before?"

"Sort of."

Here "sort of" meant "yes": I had driven a stick shift but it had only been on two occasions. The first was for three days during the shooting of an episode of *The Untouchables*; I played the doomed son of some Kentucky rum-runner and succeeded in grinding up the transmission of an antique 1929 Model A. The second was two agonizing days delivering pastries for a Russ's IGA when I was in high school.

I must learn to listen to the sounds, feel the needs of the engine, and shift when the car asks me. I promptly stall out in the middle of the intersection of 27th Street and Highway 2. But somehow I jerk and shudder and stall my way to Macy and the last day of the annual Omaha *he'dewachi*.

When we met a year ago, Susann's life was in disarray and trouble. In the two months since I last saw her, she has participated in an important "Honor the Youth Spiritual

Run." The run was held to draw attention to youth suicide among Native peoples. During the run, important things came into focus for Susann. She decided to leave her home on the reservation to live in Minneapolis for a time. There she found a circle of people who tangibly helped with the traditional Native school she hopes to build. Susann has continued to write, and during these last two months she's performed her poetry in public. She could not bring her children to Minnesota so, knowing how much they needed and missed their father, she asked that he honor his youth and take them. He did. She tells me that this is truly one of the hardest things she has ever done. To put the final point on all the change, Susann is leaving the house where they lived for the last seven years. She has returned to Macy to pack the few needed things and toss the remains. She grins as she tells me she wants nothing of what used to be because it's all forward now. "I don't know what exactly is going to happen now, but I'm ready. Hey, you want to go up to the Holy Fireplace? It's a place I'd meant to take you last summer. It's dry, so we won't get stuck."

I explain the stick shift and my difficulties. Susann says she'll risk it. "It's all forward from here, isn't it?"

As we both walk to the hilltop parking, a group of men with black "Powwow Security" t-shirts stare. I think they're staring at Susann.

"No, they're staring at you! You're not from here. They're not going to talk to us. But, you know, I'll hear about it, and my mom will, and my family will. Before the evening's out they'll know who you are and, likely, your license plate number. Staring at me? Christopher, you're funny."

We stall out five or six times on a winding ascent over

the deeply rutted dirt roads. The trees arch over the road and make it like a rich green tunnel. It takes a good half hour to get there—up onto one of the high bluffs overlooking the Missouri Valley.

>>DISPATCH: THE HOLY FIREPLACE
After the Powwow

I had imagined the picturesque: some great stone chimney in tended ruins. On first appearance the place is not that in the least. It's a small garbage can tilted against a faded sign that says,

> This Place Is Sacred. Respect Our Tradition. The Omaha Nation.

Susann disappears down the margin of the bluff. I follow. When I reach the margin, the breath is taken out of me. The view is eternal. To the south, an elbow-bend in the wide Missouri embraces billows and pillows of green. Directly to the east, what would have been an unobstructed view of the dawn, is farmland as far as the eye can see. To the north, more woods and another glimpse of the rolling river. Susann mentions that a hundred years ago the course of the Missouri changed through the valley. "We don't want things to change but they always do."

She sits down in a nest of high grass. I'm concerned that some of the weeds look an awful lot like poison sumac and recall an unfortunate Boy Scout incident that left my mother concerned I might one day be sterile. None of this do I share with Susann. I just sit on the path. "I love to come here and think. You can see where people have sat for years and years."

There are other nests of grass on the steep margin like the one in which Susann is nestled. "We can't lose sight of what's important here. The truth. The children are important and the children need the truth."

"So do I, so do adults. The story I want to tell is about trying to figure out the truth of who we are in this place."

"It's also about transformation. Not maybe on the surface. But deep down. That's why you have to struggle for it. I think that's what you're trying to say and why you've taken this journey the way you have. You've committed to this story. You made a vow. You don't even have to speak it. I know you've made it. We're trying to find the words. Our words can transform us. But I'm going to tell you this: by what you're doing you're stirring up five hundred years of anger, pain, and shame. You're bound to get some directed at you. Not everybody is going to understand. It's going to be hard, and not just to find the words. But no one is a victim here."

>>Dispatch: Challenge
August 10, 2007

It is 8:50 a.m. and I am not driving the stick shift. I am in Libby Wicks-Bailey's suv, headed back up to the Omaha Reservation. Libby is the Lied Center's liaison to the Native community, holding her job despite recent cutbacks to programming at the Lied. Libby is joyously round and explosively enthusiastic but don't think that she is anything but a force with which to be reckoned. She will think nothing of the long drives up and all-day waits, if necessary, to accomplish what she must: meeting with teachers and students, listening to troubles, building connections with the University of Nebraska and the Lied Center.

Libby has set up a meeting for me to meet with John Keegan. John has been a teacher on the Omaha Reservation for thirty-eight years and is an adopted member of the tribe. John has championed, with Libby, an upcoming performance for me in Macy.

John Keegan was born in Dublin, Ireland, almost sixty years ago. He came to the States when he was in his late teens or early twenties and soon joined America's Teacher's Corps. He was assigned to the Omaha Reservation to teach music. He has never left. He writes and orchestrates music and plays every instrument in his band room. John is an adopted nephew of Elise Leclerc. He had always wanted to act but wasn't able to muster the nerve to audition in Sioux City until he was forty-five years old. He is now part of a company of folks trying to create a theater in Walthill, Nebraska. John is wiry and a smoker. His hair is thick and once was ginger-colored, now is frosted gray. He has a beard as wiry as he is. It, too, is ginger and frost. His glasses are dirty, but not from carelessness so much as from the owner's constant motion. How could he have time to wipe them? He has a gravelly whiskey voice that in some instances carries a Native flatness and then lilts into an Irish brogue.

As Libby and I drive to Macy we talk about the plans for the rest of my visit. Libby is excited for Susann. Libby has noticed the changes. Libby and I are going to pick up Susann in Macy and bring her down to Lincoln. "She's giggling. She's actually giggling. I have never seen Susann giggle and it's just wonderful!" Libby squeals the last word and starts to giggle herself. "I just love it. I didn't expect all this. When she left William . . . well, I was afraid of her.

Oh, so afraid. But now! And you say that she and William are talking?"

"They spoke yesterday, according to Susann."

"Wonderful!" Libby squeals, and then lowers an octave to get down to business.

"Now, you're going to meet with John. They're having a meeting at the school. He wants to introduce you around and then he's going to show you over to the Valentine Center, where you'll be performing later in the month. I'll be meeting up at the tribal college and back down at the public school. When you're done you give me a call or come and find me."

"My cell doesn't work up here."

"Have John do it. After the tribal college, I have to go up to Winnebago and the Little Priest School, and after that, Walthill. I think that's supposed to be at 4:00 p.m., but who knows."

I step out of the SUV and, using the same enthusiasm that she uses as she moves through life, Libby peels out and leaves a plume of dust.

The Omaha Reservation Public School is everything: preschool, kindergarten, elementary, etc. In the wake of dust I see three women approaching. One looks familiar. Out of the corner of my eye I see Libby's SUV make an abrupt U-turn. She pulls back up as the women come nearer to where I am standing looking up at the school. Libby swings out of the door. I don't know how she's had time to put the car into park.

"Christopher!" she squeals. "This is Helen! Oh dear, I have wanted you two to meet." She catches her breath. "This is *wonderful*. Helen, this is Christopher Cartmill. He's the playwright."

"I've heard."

Her voice is deep and serious. Helen is in the front of the three women. Her face is impassive and hard. She introduces the other two: one is a cousin and the other is the cousin's or Helen's daughter or granddaughter. I can't quite make that out. The six eyes boring into me are disconcerting. The cousin wants nothing to do with me. The daughter-granddaughter is a bit more welcoming. I wish I'd heard her name. Omaha kinship is very difficult for an outsider to understand. I should have listened better. After looking me up and down, Helen turns to Libby.

"Are you coming to the Hand Game?"

"Oh, no, I'm afraid I've got to go up to the tribal college and then—Oh dear!—I should run. Hopefully I'll be back before the end. This is *good*! So good for you all to meet!"

Before any other words are exchanged, Libby zooms off in her suv leaving another cloud of dust. The cousin shouts up the hill to a well-dressed woman walking into the tribal offices across the street, "Are you coming to the Hand Game?!"

"I didn't know there was one! I'll be there!" says the well-dressed woman.

"There is something that's been concerning me about what you're doing," Helen says to me firmly. "Bright Eyes LaFlesche. She's important and always gets pushed to the background. I don't want that."

This is not a plea. This is a challenge.

"She's definitely not going to be in the background of my work," I say. She's one of the heroes. I admire her a great deal."

"That's good." Helen's face softens considerably, changing completely. "It's important to us. To her family and to all us women."

>>DISPATCH: HAND GAME
A Moment Later

I find John Keegan and he gets some teachers to move their seats so I can sit next to him. He starts to explain the rules of a Hand Game. The two teams—in this case the North and the South—sit opposite one another. One team "hides" and the other team "guesses." Two members of the "hiding" team take a pair of stones and hide them, one in each hand, while the team sings, drums, and attempts to distract the "guessing" team. The leader of the "guessing" team then has to guess which hand of the two opposing team members are holding the stones. The guessing side, in the Omaha version of the game, points an eagle feather at the hand he supposes holds the stone. If a hider is guessed, he or she must surrender the guessed stone to the opponent. The hiding side continues hiding and singing until both pairs of stones have been guessed and surrendered. The teams then reverse roles and the game continues until one team holds all the stones. The game is ancient and, by all accounts, found among many tribal cultures. The rules and complexity of the game depend on the tribe and the circumstance. Hand Games are played regularly. This one has been organized to remind the non-Native teachers of the Omaha Public School about Native culture. One of the teachers sitting next to me (a bloated-looking woman wearing a cat-embroidered jeans jacket) clearly is not interested in reminders. She is doing a newspaper crossword. The room is positively arctic cold. John and I are seated in front of the drum circle. I recognize the singers from the powwow. John instructs me on the rules and etiquette of the game. "We lost the last round so our team has to lead the round dance and gift the head table as a penalty."

Two white women from our team are given one maraca each by the emcee's assistants. Paired up, drums start and the women do the step-walk dance around the drum. They are given dollar bills from our side (the South) and must contribute their own penalty for losing, then the whole amount will be given to the head table. John informs me that this giving of dollars by the team is new to the Omahas. "Traditions change."

As the women dance and people contribute, others from our team join in. "It's a penalty but it's an honor to carry the gourds [the maracas]. After the Round Dance is done we'll have a new match. You're the new guy so they're likely to single you out."

Our side is guessing first. The drums start. John is given the eagle feather. He has a singular Hand Game style, dancing arms akimbo with the eagle feather flicking and darting above and below. Once the hiders have hidden the stones, in order to distract they are bouncing their hands up and down and side to side. John flicks the feather right or left, and elicits snickers from Natives and non-Natives alike. I can see, by the way he plays, the strategic and complex intricacies of a seemingly simple game. John's acumen has paid off. Our team, the South, has won. The guessers come to face us. The assistants come by. I am handed one of the stones. The guesser is a young white teacher. She's into it. Behind my back I wrap the stone in my right hand.

Before I can bounce my hands twice to distract, I'm caught and out of the game. The guesser then outs my partner right away. John, who is dancing around behind the guesser in order to put her off her game, gives me a wink. I sit.

Despite my weak showing, John wins it for us. Then Norman, the emcee, announces that this is the last round. One more Round Dance. I want to put my contribution in so I hand the lead dancer a dollar. John pats me on the shoulder and says, "When they come back around, why don't you get up and dance. I'll do it with you."

At the last of it we all turn to the center to honor the drum and then return to our seats. Prizes are given. John wins for being our best feather man. He later tells me that he brought the prizes, so I guess what goes around comes around. The emcee announces it is time for lunch. They place a blanket in the center of the room. "It's traditional that guests bring their own dishes and utensils," John tells me as he lifts a bag out from under his chair. "But you're a guest so you're not expected to. I brought you some."

"You can all eat! Even though you dance like you was Cherokees." Norman laughs at his own joke, a joke that no one else acknowledges, except John.

I ask John what it means to "dance like a Cherokee."

"Dance like a white man."

"Oh."

While we're feasting, Norman invites anyone who wants to speak to speak. This is also an Omaha tradition. Helen gets the microphone first. She speaks for about twenty minutes, touching on the same subjects multiple times.

Thanks to the singers and drum.
>   Thanks to Norman and Flora and the elders.
>   Thanks to Vida for organizing this.

Thanks to the teachers for teaching their children. Their children might seem difficult but they are in need of help and therefore she is grateful.

Thanks to the new teachers.

The Omaha ways are important.

The subtlety of variations on the themes interests me. Like most seemingly random thought-parades, a structure does exist: they always start and end with gratitude and gratitude is peppered throughout. No one will interrupt the speaker or tell her to move it along; it's her time. The meat of the meaning is revealed somewhere close to the three-quarters-in part. Rambling is not a fault. Economy of effort is not a value. Whatever it takes you to get there is what it takes. Eloquence is not about "how" you say it, but "what" you say. I think the non-Natives in the house have tuned out. The only ones responding are Native. After Helen finishes, the well-dressed woman who Helen called down from the tribal center speaks:

My thanks to the singers and the drum. My thanks to Norman and Flora. Thanks to Helen, for what she said. Thanks to all of you teachers. The new ones, thank you. I just heard there was a Hand Game and got told to come. So I did. Thank you. You must hear what Helen said. Our children are important. We trust them to you. I would like to see more Native faces out there, but I don't. But thank you anyway. You must respect our ways and understand that our children must learn. They must learn to be a part of the mainstream culture but they must learn that they are Omaha. You have to make them come. Most of the time they don't want to come. My children are grown but they hated school. I don't expect you to entertain them but they must want to come. You are not Omaha but we have trusted our Omaha children to you.

She continues with more thanks and repetition but I am stunned by the undercurrent of anger with which she says all this, and how easily her message is ignored by all the feasting teachers. She clearly intended her words to be bracing. The lunch ends.

>>Dispatch: The Shelter of Storms
Immediately Following

A few days earlier Susann had told me that her aunt, Marguerite Baker, the tribal leader, wanted to see me. When lunch is finished I tell John that I need to go up to tribal headquarters and see if Ms. Baker is there. I tell John that I'll be back soon. "Christopher, remember, you can never count on soon. She might not be there."

Crossing over to the tribal center I see behind it some dark, dark, iron-gray clouds. "Is Marguerite Baker in?"

"Go around there and ask one of the women at the desks." I do just that and one of the women gets up and walks to a far door and softly knocks.

"Christopher! Come in. Let me see you."

Marguerite has her hair down and looks very young and energized. "Not a handshake! A hug for you!"

"So, how have you been?" I ask.

"Ah, well. Busy. Busy. I'm hoping I can come to your performance thing later in the month," she says, flipping a calendar without really looking at it. "Oh, yes. That is the day, isn't it? I might have to be in California."

"For pleasure?"

"It's never pleasure. It's all work. Then Reno. You remember the casino negotiations. It's never-ending. Ah, well. Oh, I've still been telling people how you just captured me.

My son was just in New York." She picks up the phone. "Would Stephen Baker come to the offices? Right away."

Her face loses the kind smile and she jumps right into a subject that is clearly important to her. "I've been talking with Susann all morning. Her mother wanted me to. I don't think she should leave. Her mother has been crying. I think she's running away. I told you that when I first came from Lincoln—for two years—I cried. My son did, too. But this is home. Susann shouldn't turn her back on her people."

"I don't think that's how she's thinking."

"It's hard, yes. But we need her. We need her talent. We need her energy. She's just been through a hard time and needs to face her life here."

I am getting the meaning that I am expected to talk to Susann for Marguerite. I'm wondering if they think that I may have instigated Susann's move to Minneapolis.

"She's leaving with you."

"No. Well—just to go to Lincoln. She's not going to Minneapolis, she tells me, 'til September."

"She shouldn't go. I can't demand she stay. But I think she must. This is a mistake."

At that, Stephen enters and saves the day. Marguerite's demeanor switches. We talk about New York. How expensive it is. How the Queens Native powwow was a bust for Stephen. How overwhelming the city was for him. I tell him to let me know when he comes again. Suddenly, Susann rushes breathlessly into the room.

"I've been looking everywhere for you, Christopher! Finally. I have one more load out at the house."

Obtusely, I ask if she needs my help. With her jaw clenched she says, "Yes. It shouldn't take—we need to go!

We need to go now!" Quick good-byes to Stephen and Marguerite, who hugs me and says in my ear, "She shouldn't go."

I'm about a hundred steps behind Susann, who is already out the door. By the time I catch up and get outside she is already in her van and driving around to get me. The car is stuffed with boxes and smells like cats. Susann is still breathing hard.

"Are you okay?"

"No. It's been a bad day. My mom has been crying for days, telling me I'm abandoning her, and then she gets Marguerite to talk to me. I was there for about three hours while I got told I'm doing something stupid. I know this is not stupid! I need to do this. I'm not abandoning anyone. It's black and white with them. They can't even see because they're so caught up in their own feelings. I need to get out of here. It's funny. I've been here, what, a month, and they choose now to say all this. We have to get the rest of my stuff out of the house and into the van, then I can be done with it."

"They love you and only want the best for you."

"But I know what's best. They just won't listen."

"Remember, you can't be a prophet in your own hometown."

The instant we pull onto the gravel driveway of Susann's old house, the heavens open up and the rain starts coming down in sheets. The house is not as near to empty as I'd assumed, which is apparent as we walk in out of the torrential rain. Susann points to a few items in plastic containers. "Those go! There's a chest out on the porch; that goes."

The chest weighs over a hundred pounds, by the looks of it. I get to work. I brace myself against the rain as I load stuff into the back of the van. I lean into the wet. Susann keeps finding more and more in the house that has to go. FLASH! BANG! POP! The lightning and thunder is terrifying. I think that either of us could get struck at any moment. Susann is gathering things and I'm running back and forth in and out of the rain. The van is so heavily loaded that I fear it may not make it back to Macy. The rain begins to pour into the van from gaps in windows and doors.

"There's always one more thing when you move," I shout over the rush of rain as we're wrestling the hundred-pound chest into the van. FLASH! CRASH! Whew, that was close.

We both dash back into the house. The sound of the rain on the roof is unbearably loud. Susann shouts that there is something she must do. I don't understand. She steps into the center of the room and pulls out some cedar and sage from her wet pockets. She quiets herself. She then goes room to room, burning the cedar and sage.

I let her alone to bless, cleanse, and say good-bye to her old home. I stand just outside the front door, half in the rain. Susann announces that she has found more books in her old office. I run the books out to the van. More water is pouring onto all the boxes and books inside. When I get back into the house, Susann has gone to the basement. I hadn't noticed before that there even was a basement. I wait as the storm continues around us. She finally comes to the door and stands looking back into the house. I step out onto the porch and into the rain to leave her alone in the house for a final time.

The rain is coming down so hard I can't see any of the fields across the way. I can hear Susann praying, though, like a conversation overheard in another room. She steps out of the house and takes a moment there. "Seven years. I'm not crying now. Wow. I don't need to."

Together we dash to the van. I get in and really take in how wet I am, how wet everything is. It suddenly begins to hail. The sky is letting go with the works. Susann gets in, but has to run back out because she's left the keys in the door.

Susann backs the van out and the sound of hail on the van pops and startles. The windshield of the van is already cracked. The hail is coming down so heavy it could make it worse, I think. I can't see the road because the passenger's side wiper is broken and makes a "T" that wicks away nothing. The dirt road is now a fast-moving stream that looks as though it could carry us down.

"Quite a sign, isn't it?" Susann shouts over the thunder and hail.

"The final obstacle!" I say.

"Not an obstacle! This is the way the grandfather who named me talks to me. Always!"

"What's he saying?"

"A lot!"

We drive on and, honest to God, the moment we get back into Macy the rain stops, the clouds part, and by the time Susann is dropping me off in front of the school the sun is out and shining. I can see that Susann is now about to cry.

>>DISPATCH: THERE'S A HOLE IN MY MOCCASIN

August 13, 2007

The Lied Center has generously given me an apartment in downtown Lincoln but, ungenerously, the place is a synthetic cherry–scented ward of depression. The bed, whose mattress I have forcibly chosen not to notice, is stained with something like blood and creaks at the slightest move. It slopes down, as if I'm going to be dropped into something. The lights from the Embassy Suites across the way give a constant yellow glow to the room. I can't sleep!

12:00 a.m. I have a disjointed dream I can't remember.

1:22 a.m. I wake with the image of a bloated toad-like psychiatrist laughing.

1:38 a.m. I note the times I wake up.

2:35 a.m. Awake, I think I see a flash of lightning, but when I look out the window I see stars. I read.

3:17 a.m. I hear voices out on the street that sound as though they are in the room, and yet I am six flights up. I read more.

Finally, I watch dawn creep in on the ceiling and the night passes.

I have an appointment at Starbucks to meet Diane wawe'nohi from the Ponca community at 8:00 a.m. She calls Starbucks her morning office. I ran into her on the street on my first day in town and we made the appointment then. I brush my teeth, put on a hat, and walk the block over.

Diane is not there, but I have a book to keep me occupied—*Bright Eyes: The Story of Susette LaFlesche, an Omaha Indian* by Dorothy Clarke Wilson. It's a first edition, signed by the author, whose photo on the back cover makes her looks very grandmotherly. I got the book for fifteen dollars at a great used bookstore in Lincoln. The tone of the book interests me. It is novelistic and grandmotherly, too.

Diane arrives. I put the book away. Diane, by dint of her personal strength, character, and charm, is very well placed in political circles, both Native and non-Native. It fascinates me that she rarely takes her eyes from the floor and only occasionally makes eye contact with me, or anyone else, for that matter, so far as I have witnessed. I fleetingly note it again and wonder at it.

We talk about the Ponca Restoration Act of 1990, which gave the Poncas back their tribal status after it was stripped in the 1960s. During the sixties and seventies the U.S. government was making a strong effort to force Native tribes and any remnants of tribal sovereignty disappear. How better to do that than to make the tribes themselves disappear? Small tribes like the Poncas were easy targets for erasure. But in 1989 or 1990, with Standing Bear as their standard and on their letterhead, a successful effort was made to reinstate the Poncas—the ones who had returned with Standing Bear and after—as the Northern Ponca Tribe. Diane is justifiably proud of this effort and her own part in the effort to give her people voice.

Diane tells me about a panel she's setting up: Standing Bear and the Law. My impression is that Diane wants very much for Chief Standing Bear to be something like a corporate logo, an image of justice, a fixed icon. The way she is trying to brand the man makes me sad, but I cannot help feeling that her heart is in the right place.

Diane tells me that she recently gave a baby gift to some friends, a white couple who'd just had a boy. She wanted to give them some Native baby moccasins. She sent out to somewhere for someone to make them. They arrived and she noticed a hole in the bottom. This concerned her and she contacted the maker. He told her that the flaw was intentional. Diane said the explanation was long but she gathered the rationale for keeping the hole was so as not to rival the perfection of Wakonda, the Great Spirit. Diane had never heard of such a thing and laughed. I told her that I'd heard of weavers who purposely drop a stitch or a weave in order to not anger God by creating something perfect. But I think my friend has heard the story wrong. I remember a passage in the book in front of us. I pretend to seek it out, but I don't want to embarrass Diane with appearing to correct her or the moccasin maker. I find it but I keep it to myself.

> Grandmother smiled, "No, Tushpáha. There's no hole in the bottom as in your baby moccasins. Do you know why we cut the hole in them?" The child shook her head. "It was so that if a messenger should come from the spirit world and say to you, 'I have come for you,' you would answer, 'I cannot go on a journey. See, my moccasins are worn out.' But now that the turning time has come, you will be prepared for the journey of life, and, please Wakonda, it will be a long one."

Diane continues: "I thought the hole was too much. I sewed it up quite a bit. I didn't feel I could give them to my friends with that gaping hole."

As we were walking out of Starbucks I said to Diane, "I understand that you have some thoughts about what I've been writing. You're welcome to share those concerns with me."

She looks at the ground. All I had heard from Libby was that the concerns were for Susann. Was Susann being cared for in the process? All that Diane had ever said to me was that she thought I'd nailed the place and time. Spoken truth with respect. This is not what she says now. "I don't see the connection between what you're doing or Susann's story and the Standing Bear story. I'm just not getting it. We'll have to wait for the next play, the one that really deals with Standing Bear. Doesn't it? I'm concerned that your stories perpetuate the image of the pitiable Indian. I don't think the children have been thought of here."

"What?"

"Susann's children. There's no doubt you're a gifted writer, but those children can only think of themselves as victims."

"I would never want that. I would never . . ."

"My concern is that the piece puts the children in danger and perpetuates the idea that all Indians are victims."

"You know that I would never . . ."

At this point, if she'd been looking at me, she would have seen that the blood had left my head.

>>Dispatch: Not Everyone Is Right
Later in the Afternoon

I drive over to Libby's house south of town, where Susann is staying while in town. I keep stalling out the stick shift. Libby's house is as lovely on the inside as she is. There is a joyful clutter of toys on the living room's blond wood floor. Susann takes me into a quiet side office, which is apparently acting as a guest room. She sits me down on a sofa and takes a seat behind the desk. She leans in toward me and speaks softly and firmly: "First of all, I'm going to tell you this again: by what you're doing you're stirring up five hundred years of anger, pain, and shame. I told you. And you will get some directed at you. Second, I want you to consider the source. You hear me? You're a good listener. Listen for what she really wants. Diane doesn't know the way. When I first met her she was a white woman. She doesn't know me. She doesn't know my children. But isn't this the way?

Yes? Pit Native against Native? Woman against woman? It's what you're stirring up. I spoke to the kids this morning. They're happy. They're with their father. I spoke with William. He says they're happy. I can hear it. I've spent a year grieving and fighting. That's done. I've protected my children from so much, but I never lied to them. They would ask me, "Mom, when are we leaving this place?" I'd say, "I don't know but you've got to be prepared. It's coming. It'll come fast and the changes will pile up. We've got to be ready." We're all ready. Not everybody is going to understand that. My mother doesn't. I've prayed and I've gotten answers. As for you, I told you that there would be sacrifices. I have been gentle with you. But this might be nothing compared with the criticism you will get. Get your shield. Like this, they're going to find where you're vulnerable. Remember that you always have a choice, and not everyone is right, and not everyone is good. You know how to listen, but do you know when to stop? You need to talk to my brother, Sam."

"From the graduation?"

"He'll understand. Call him."

>>Dispatch: Sam

August 15, 2007

I meet with Sam in the morning. He's waiting for me at that Lincoln coffee mecca, The Mill. He is bearded, gruff, and wise-looking, even when seated at a tiny café table wearing a t-shirt with wolf puppies on it and sipping fizzy fruit soda. I sit across from him and he crosses his arms over his belly. "Don't worry about Susann. I've known her a long time. And I meant what I said about you performing a healing, and I meant on those kids. Look, here, before anything more. Pick the ones that matter—whose opinions matter. You discern. Hold to those. Because lots of others will come for you now."

"Why now?"

"Because now you're putting it out into the world."

He looks deep into my eyes. He looked to me, in hindsight, like a great owl. This soon will reveal itself to be an apt image. "You know this. You put yourself out there a lot. You've got courage all over you. But you've got to learn to protect yourself."

Sam, you will remember, is a Vietnam vet. He was born in Nebraska on a farm in the center of the state. He was going to be a preacher. Vietnam changed him. He's been on a spiritual quest ever since. This is no New Age seeker of quick fixes and trendy answers. He had mystical experiences as a child. One, he tells me, involved a great horned owl. There is so much to our conversation it is hard to get things to land.

"There is blue all around you. Blue is the color of communication. This is about that, isn't it?" Sam reiterated almost all of what Susann had said to me. Everything takes on a comfortable yet mysterious tone. He starts to look more and more like that great kind owl from his story.

"You're on a journey. But this journey will have an end. There will come a time when this will be done. Let it be your choice. Don't hold onto it too long."

"But I've just started."

"Really?"

I tell him that I've decided not to go up to Niobrara for the Ponca powwow. It may not be the politically smart thing to do, but I can't drive up four hours and stay for two days when I've got so much to do. The Lied wants a reading of the second play in two weeks. His response doesn't match my practical tone.

"Good. What you're doing is dangerous."

"Dangerous?"

"Yes."

"Physically?"

"Could be, but not just that. It's dangerous what you're doing. Be certain to take care of yourself."

It is midnight, and a year ago I wish I had had a hole in my moccasin. When the messenger came from the spirit world I'd have just said, "I can't go on this journey. See, my moccasin is worn out."

>>Dispatch: Contemplating Reverse
August 19, 2007

I am still having trouble getting the hang of the stick shift. To be fair, I do have my James Bond moments—a downshift that makes music and sweet, sweet love to the car and the road—but they are only moments. In an instant I go from feeling like James Bond to feeling as if I am that ninety-year-old man in a hat who should have his license and car taken away. I've been given the finger twice, at least as far as I know. I stall out at the intersection of Highways 2 and 77, through three signal cycles. But the hardest thing— and what seems to be an idiosyncrasy of the car—is that reverse is difficult, if not impossible, to find. This has necessitated parking only where it's possible to go forward. I cannot drive into a driveway to turn around. You see, I must always go forward.

The NET documentarian, Karen Fox, wants to get together to discuss our projects. Her Standing Bear Project has failed to receive funding from the National Endowment for the Humanities; she tells me she dropped into a funk over the loss. I drive around the NET parking lot for twenty minutes to find a spot that doesn't require backing out.

"You look tired," she says, as I take a seat in her office. It's been a long year for Karen and she can see it's been a long two weeks for me. We warm up with more Standing Bear talk. She's anxious to hear about what I've got going and anxious to share with me her new approach to the documentary on Standing Bear. But first she knows I need to vent. You'd expect someone in Karen's profession to "interview." She does not do this, but she makes it easy for me to talk and is genuinely interested. I suppose that's the best interview technique there is. I tell her about my Starbucks exchange.

"But you've got to remember what's at stake," she says. "They want a place at the table."

"And who am I to take their story?"

"You've got to take into consideration what these people you're talking to are bringing to it. Every one of them has an idea of what the story should be and who gets to tell it. It's personal. It's like my documentary now—how I've planned it. It starts on the statue of Standing Bear in Ponca City, Oklahoma. Ironically, a twenty-two-foot icon rising in a place Standing Bear wanted desperately to leave."

"But then this man becomes an icon. Here's the logo for Standing Bear, Inc. Is this," I wonder, "what people want? Does this make up for all the struggle and pain, the miles, the loss, the personal and cultural devastation? What does this really say about Standing Bear's own sacrifice and struggle, his freedom and his courage? What does it really say about the freedom and courage of Susann Cloud Horse or my friend at Starbucks?"

August 18, 2007

I have been invited to participate in a sweat lodge ceremony.

I gather my stuff for the sweat: towel, shorts, change of shirt. We get into the stick shift car and drive out by the state penitentiary. Susann knows the way but she can't seem to recognize the landmarks. Now remember, I am having trouble getting the car into reverse so we have to make wide circles. After about an hour of ever-widening circles Susann gets more and more anxious that we are truly lost. We double-back, but always driving forward. Unfortunately, I choose to head down a dirt road that turns out to be a flat dead end with a ravine in front and a ravine to one side and a bank of cedars to the other side. Reversing is the only option. But I can't. We both get out and try to push the car backward. "Why is it always like this? Why does it have to be so hard?" I finally let out with some frustration.

Susann says, "I think there's *heyoka* energy in this. In fact, I know it."

Heyoka is a Lakota way. A *heyoka* is one who does things backward or opposite. The way is to remind us that we are merely human and not to become too serious about ourselves—not to imagine we are more powerful than we are. Wakonda, the Great Spirit, chooses who is *heyoka*. It's a difficult path. The Cloud Horse children are *heyoka*. Sam had told me this back in May and Susann has spoken of it a couple of times. I've never before known what to make of it. Now I have a better understanding of the concept.

"This is a *heyoka* car. Definitely!" Susann laughs and starts walking around to see if we can at all go forward.

I am not laughing, not anymore. I try again. I lurch the

car forward, closer to going into the ravine. I'm thinking about how I am going to explain this *heyoka* energy to the folks at the Lied when we have to get the car they have lent me towed out of a ravine near the state pen.

Susann is now fifty yards out into the weeds, praying. Her back is toward me and visible in my rearview mirror. Something happens. The silliness of all this hits me. I relax and laugh. Just then, like warmed butter on toast, the stick catches into reverse and I back out toward Susann. She turns around, doubles over, and laughs out loud. We both can't stop laughing. Back in the car, and now ready and capable of moving forward, Susann says, "The *heyoka* spirits are asking, How bad do we want to go to this sweat lodge? Is tonight the night? Do you really need this? It's our choice; they just want to make sure we're making the right choice."

>>DISPATCH: THE SWEAT LODGE
Sometime in the Evening of the Same Day
TIME HAS LOST ALL MEANING

I am in the fetal position on the matted floor of a roughly four-foot-high, twenty-foot-round dome of blankets and canvas—an authentic Native sweat lodge. No New-Age-Hippie-Dippie-Faux-Native-Culture-Tour-Stop this. It is hardcore and hot, heavy medicine. I am gasping for air from the only place to take it from, the floor. The strong smell of wet earth being cooked pushes up my nostrils. It is completely black. I know that if anyone could see me I'd look, for all the world, like a guppy: wide-eyed and panting on a tabletop, having jumped from the bowl. There is drumming and singing. I'm hearing what I think is the third round of prayer. The singing begins to warp in my head.

I swear I am listening to a hymn tune that I know. I find I want to sing along.

Lead Kindly Light, amid th'encircling gloom;
Lead thou me on!

But all that seems to come out is a monotone low moan.

The night is dark, and I am far from home.

I know that tune, I think. I raise both arms up into the searing air. *I know that tune! We used to sing it in Sunday School. Didn't we?*

I do not ask to see the distant scene . . .

My hands I know are swaying as if I'm a Pentecostal. *Why are my arms in the air?* I can feel my arms in the infernal heat. *That's a hymn tune. Isn't it?*

. . . one step enough for me!

With last bangs of the drum I shout out, or think I shout out, a loud . . .

Amen!

Once it's out of my mouth, the word and my arms drop to the ground like sandbags and I'm once again gasping for air that doesn't burn. But when the front flap is opened (for what I think is the third time) I rise up to sitting so as not to be seen writhing on the ground. Above me, on the thick blankets that make the hide of the lodge, I see for the first time the images of horses running. Three of them, heading east. I want to lie back down, but I force myself to keep up and show my spirit.

Susann and I finally find the sweat lodge grounds. The sky is baby pink and baby blue; the air is heavy and older. Since there is no breeze, the trees are silent. I try to find a place to park from which I will not have to drive in reverse. This is impossible. There are vans and pickups all around in what is a fairly small opening in a bank of cottonwoods and cedar trees. Accept. Park now, reverse later.

We step out into the pink heavy air. Susann is still laughing at the stick shift car and our adventures in *heyoka* energy. I've gotten serious and can't seem to let go of anything—not reverse, not my week, not this project, not the questions about why I am even doing all this. I don't know if I am ready for this ceremony—for it is clearly another test. This is a test that I've assigned myself. I had every opportunity to turn back. The car was even helping in the decision. Susann would have thought nothing of it had I wanted to turn back. But I'm an accepting if not free spirit.

The sweat lodge grounds and compound were created by Sam, the Great Horned Owl, and his adopted Lakota brethren. I had heard from Sam that they recently held a Sun Dance ceremony here. A Sun Dance is deep medicine. Each tribe has its differences, but here there is dancing, singing, praying, drumming, fasting, and ritual piercing of the chest and back. The object of the piercing is to sacrifice one's self to the Great Spirit. Connected to the tree of life by straps and small pegs, pierced through in places on the chest or back, a man runs or leans back and breaks the connection. A Sun Dancer has to commit to four years of dancing. It's a sacrifice for one's family and community. It's not the same for women. As with all things, I am still learning. The ceremony was made illegal in the United States in 1880, one year after the Standing Bear trial. It was finally allowed again when President Jimmy Carter signed a law reinstating the freedom for Native peoples to worship in this way.

I can feel the energy all around the little clearing in the cottonwoods and cedar. It is heavy with anticipation and loose concentration. I can feel it. I am in awe and not a little trepidatious. It's dangerous, Sam said. Is this dangerous? Was something planned for me here?

A few yards from where I park the car, two tents that look like giant Portobello mushroom caps are on the grass. In front of them is a deep firepit of granite blocks making a wall that goes down about five feet into the earth. The heat from the fire and the rocks in the coals shimmer in the hot blue and pink air. A shirtless Native man is tending the fire. There are picnic tables under the collection of trees that lead to a nearby copse of cottonwoods bordering what I think is the margin of a creek. Scattered among the tables and trees are lawn chairs. Away from this scene, but still nearby, is an authentic plains tepee. Made of hide, the tepee stands a good fifteen feet. The tops of the long poles are splayed out like a pianist's fingers into the now-purpling sky. Hidden in among the trees and just a bit beyond is a much larger structure. I get the impression that it is a tribal longhouse but I don't go there to check it out. Things are getting under way.

It is obvious that the man tending the fire has Sun Danced before, as evidenced by the two nearly symmetrical scars welted on his chest. The same can be said of almost all the men I see. A good half of those waiting for the ceremony are non-Native. A few of these, I am told, are work release inmates from the state penitentiary. Sam has made an arrangement with the prison system: they use Native teachings to help the inmates keep off drugs and straighten out their lives. I am wishing Sam were here. I think I could use his protection. No one is talking to me. Susann is meeting the people she knows. She is talking to Techu, the leader of the sweat. She pulls me over to meet him. Techu smiles and takes my hand. He makes a simple and unadorned welcome. At this, a small wiry man with long, wavy jet black hair introduces himself: Greco. Greco seems very kind. Once I am introduced, everyone unceremoniously continues his or her preparations. Susann goes to help. I retire to the background to watch.

At both lodges, altars are being set and prepared. At the altar between the main lodge and the firepit a buffalo skull is laid in a dirt circle surrounded by rocks. The entrance to the lodge, a flap lifted up and over, is a little more than two feet wide. The other mushroom tent to the north is smaller and has a similar altar, but the people there are further along in its preparation. An elderly woman in a calico dress is praying at the altar, while a slightly younger man plays the drums. She is mouthing a prayer and lifting the sacred pole and pipes.

At the lodge altar the men are wondering aloud whether the rocks are ready. In preparation for this sweat I read that the rocks are spiritually activated by the fire. A short Native woman in khaki shorts (who looks as if she could be a schoolteacher) seems to be acting as Techu's assistant. She is filling large orange plastic buckets with water and hauling them to the mouth of the tent. The men are arranging the altar. The sacred pole is placed with accompanying prayers. Eagle feathers are attached with similar care. Some people have begun to stand in anticipation. The men are all shirtless, the women fully clothed in shirts and skirts. Each person has a towel. I brought a towel from the grandmotherly apartment. Without official notice, everyone seems to know that things are starting. Susann comes and tells me she will see me after the sweat is over. She walks forward to stand with the women. I'm back among a line of about fifteen men. I turn around and the man behind me has a long black beard and serial-killer eyes. His arms are heavily tattooed. I smile, say nothing, then turn back. A Native man steps in front of the altar. He apparently is someone that Susann knows well. I observe them talking. The man steps onto a small dirty carpet in front of the altar at the entrance to the lodge. Susann looks back at me and motions that I should take off my flip-flops. I do, stepping to the side. When I return to my place in line I hear Greco, who's in front of me, say to another man, "He's making a flesh sacrifice."

I look up to see Techu making small cuts in the arm of Susann's friend as he stands facing the altar. I think he is using a surgical scalpel. Five cuts are made, starting at the bottom of the shoulder and extending down to just above the elbow. Blood mixed with sweat is running down the man's arm. I get mightily concerned. Are we all to do this before the sweat? Am I expected to allow this to be done to me before I can enter the lodge? I look expectantly toward Susann. Susann doesn't look back. I'm wishing she would. The man, his ritually inflicted wounds now covered, thanks Techu with a handshake and walks around to stand between me and the bearded man with serial-killer eyes. I don't look back. An older non-Native woman steps up. She takes off her long-sleeved shirt to reveal a sleeveless t-shirt. She is going to allow the same to be done to her. I am getting more convinced that I was purposely not told I would have to make a flesh sacrifice. I feel woozy but I keep watching. It's all very strange in and among this rustic authentic setting. Techu removes another sterilized scalpel from a sealed medical wrapper. If this is going to happen to me, I'm pleased that it's all medically safe. Still, it looks strange. I am feeling light-headed. The woman doesn't flinch as Techu makes five or more small incisions in her upper arm. There are mumbled prayers.

Greco says to the man in front of me, "She's doing this for her family." I remember something Susann had said to me a number of times during the previous week: "When we pray, we never pray for ourselves. We always pray for others. That's what we are called to do by our tradition."

As the woman shakes Techu's hand, a river of blood and sweat pours down her arm. Another woman covers it with gauze. The woman is beaming with love and soulfulness. She takes her place among the group of women gathered near the entrance to the lodge.

The small woman acting as Techu's second uses a stick to bring to the altar a tin with filled with hot smoking coals from the firepit. A bundle of sage is thrown into the tin. The first woman in line is signaled to enter the lodge. I won't have to be cut! Aah! I relax. The first woman enters the lodge on her knees. She does so not just because that is all the entrance can accommodate; no, it is an act of humbling penance. She is followed by the others. Everyone is taking the smoke from the tin and wafting it onto their faces. Techu hands each one of us a stem of sage. I follow suit when my turn comes.

I crawl into the dark dank heat. We enter into the lodge

and move to the left, then swing around to our places, just like the dance around the powwow circle. Slightly off-center and closer to the door is a shallow round pit of stone. There is no hole in the ceiling above. I catch sight of Susann. She mouths that I should take off my belt. I forgot. I quickly do so while also trying to find a spot of real estate on the floor of the more crowded men's section. I am backed up against the shallowly curved wall of the tepee; the structure is made of blankets and canvas supported by arches of wooden and metal heavy rods in a widely spaced basket pattern. Techu welcomes the newcomers. We are asked to raise our hands. Three of us. Techu gives us the ground rules: "You may leave. No one will think less of you. Just ask permission of the relatives." He says something in Lakota. Then he repeats, "Just ask permission of the relatives. You can come back in but only when they let you know outside. You have to move this direction around to leave." He points to the way we came in. "Whatever you do, never stand up. Never. It'll be hot up there." I observe that there's not much "up" up there. "It'll be dark in here, so watch where you put your arms and legs. You're bound to get on somebody. Bring 'em in!"

Techu motions, then through the small entry appears a man with a pitchfork, carrying a large rock taken from what I can only suppose is the firepit. I now know the rocks are spiritually activated by the fire. The energized rock is set down. A very tall and imposing man named Ed, who I found out earlier lives in part of Sam's basement, picks up the hot rock using two stag's horns and places it into the small lodge pit. This ritual happens twenty-one more times. Each time a big rock is brought in, Techu and the other men laugh and say that it should count for two. "Oh man, this is going to be a hot one!" Susann catches my wide eyes and winks.

It might have been after the third round of prayers, drumming, and singing when the flap of canvas opens and light streams into the pitch black of the squat tent. Unidentifiable hands place a couple more orange buckets inside the tent. Men twice or three times my size are prostrate around me, gasping. Three people have dropped out after the first round of the zealous sweltering heat. One man, a couple of bodies over, is muttering prayers that sound like pleadings for mercy. The women were draped down onto blankets. I look over at Susann and her head is bowed. She looks like she has aged thirty years. I lift myself up and see the unidentifiable hands pass Techu a charcoal-black buffalo horn. Techu dips the horn into one of the orange buckets. He passes it to his right to one of the women. She takes it and drinks it down. Techu, I can see, is a veteran of many a Sun Dance ritual. On his chest is a cascade of scars and welts from piercings past. He's smiling and making jokes I can't remember.

"Water'll never taste so good." This, I think, is like the Eucharist—Communion. Passed back to Techu for refills, the buffalo horn makes its way around the tent. Techu uses this time to give the service's sermon. "At times like these you've got to know that—in times like these . . ."

I'm watching the horn and hoping it will get around to me before the flaps close and the drumming and heat come up again. "You have got to know that . . . there might not seem to be a way to turn back, but you can." Did he just say what I thought he said? "There might not seem to be a way to turn back, but there is. If your path has been chosen for you . . ."

His words rise up with the steam as one of the men in front of me pours what would have been his share of water onto the rocks. A searing billow of steam rises and mushrooms out over us all.

I begin to ponder, "Techu?" I know that name. Don't I? From something? If it's what I think, Techu is another name for the Egyptian god Thoth—god of magic, wisdom, and time, messenger and interpreter of the gods. I'm wondering if this is the etymology of his name? Is he Egyptian? No. Is that also a Sioux name? Strange thoughts.

This line of wondering falls away as my arms seem to want to give out on me. Techu invites everyone to speak their prayers. One man confesses that he'd been tempted to use drugs that very afternoon but chose not to. He wants to pray for the men who'd tempted him and then used. One of the drummers says that he's been separated from his children because of his job. He starts to cry. I look over and see that Susann is crying. The man says he wants to pray for his children and their mother. He wants them to understand that he had to make a choice and the choice was for them. One man wants to say a prayer of thanks for this sweat and the friends who support him. All this is both searingly clear and honest and a rambling blur of confession and hoped-for absolution. This is like church, I think. Susann speaks up in support of the man who'd had to leave his kids. She says she knows. She does. She asks for prayers for her children. She prays for her family, that her family might understand her choices. Finally, she asks for prayers for me and the words I make. She prays that I will be protected and open. That I will see my choices as choices. Another man dumps his water onto the hot rocks and another billow of hot steam rushes over us. The praying continues but I turn inward.

I pray silently for Susann's children and Susann's safety and choices. I pray in gratitude. I pray for Standing Bear, his people. My people. I pray for Diane wawe'nohi. I pray for my friends and . . . I pray for my family . . . all families . . . by blood and by choice. I pray for enduring all trials, for finding a way . . . for finding a way home.

The unidentified hands remove the buckets. I place my towel over my head. I can see through it that the light is leaving the place. The drumming and the singing starts up and I fall back onto the floor like a dropped rag. As the last light escapes I look up and see the forms of those three horses above my head. Three horses running. Three. What could that mean? Blackness. Vows. I made a vow to see this through. I've seen it through, in part. Three parts. Three horses. Three plays.

"You have fulfilled one vow." It's not that I hear it spoken in the dark. I hear it coming up from inside me. I have fulfilled one vow. Which vow? "You'll know. But you now have to decide if you will make another." Another? "You'll know. Tell Susann. She'll need to hear this." Was the vow to her? "You'll know." This is when the singing begins to warp in my head. I swear I can hear that hymn tune again. I try to sing along.

> I was not ever thus, nor prayed that Thou shouldst lead me on;

> But, of course, I just moan.

> I loved to choose and see my path; but now lead Thou me on!

> Both arms go up and into the searing air.

I loved the garish day, and,
spite of fears . . .

I'm moan-singing! The last cadence of the drums and the shrill singing halt and I exclaim, "Amen!"

The unidentified hands again lift the tent flaps to let in the light. The sun has gone down so the light is blue-gray and cool. Techu laughs and says that big things have happened. Susann is still looking like her own great-great-grandmother. Ed, the seneschal, motions that we should all circle the walls of the lodge. I drag myself back against the steeply curved incline of the tent wall. I look up at the fabric of the tenting; it must have been an old sleeping bag. On it are three green horses running. Techu pours the rest of the water from the buckets onto the rocks.

The sacred prayer pipes are passed in by the hands. Each pipe has been provided by someone attending the lodge, in honor of their prayers. The prayer pipes move counter-clockwise round the circle. Techu is *heyoka*. Everything in reverse.

I don't smoke. I never have smoked. That's not quite true, I've had to smoke twice onstage (though those weren't really cigarettes) and once (with the real thing) when I was in graduate school. I thought I needed to be cooler and try, but it turned out I just got immediately, wretchedly sick. And right now there are as least twelve prayer-pipes making their way around the circle to me. I cannot let them pass me by. These are prayers. The first one comes and I take a drag, but nothing. A bearded man next to me taps me on the shoulder to let me know the tobacco is not lit. He relights it for me. I take a deep drag. I thought I would have been made ill, but, no. This is prayer. I take each pipe in turn. The pipe-smoking lasts for what seems an hour. The bearded man next to me has to relight at least half of the pipes I smoke. He is very kind and nonjudgmental about it. I don't think I have the hang of it.

As the last pipe finishes its round, Techu laughs again and motions that we must leave. In reverse. Men first. We round out. As I pass Techu he says,

"Seems like Jesus made a visit to us, today. He had his trials."

I crawl out and step up into the navy blue of dusk. Before anything, I make for the water. It never has tasted so good or so sweet. Folks are setting out food on long tables. It's so dark out that what kind of food it is is anyone's guess. Susann sets off to change. I go to the car and put on a dry shirt. I didn't bring other shorts so I have to sit in the sweat-saturated pair I have on. I risk the darkness and get some food. I can't tell beans from potato salad or slaw from barbeque beef. I get it anyway. I'm very hungry. I sit down alone at a picnic table near the small stream. I can only tell it's near the stream because I hear it. The authentic tepee is looming over to the left—all shadow and indigo above it. Tangled in the support poles of the tepee is a toenail crescent moon—bright and airy silver. It's pretty much our only light by now. Ed, the seneschal, sits down at the table across from me. He is a large man, with large hands. The whites of his eyes glow like the moon.

"Beautiful, isn't it? I remember my first sweat. This was a good one. Hot. By the fourth round. . . ."

"There were four rounds? I only remember three."

"Wild, isn't it?"

Things break up pretty quickly. Susann and I finish wolfing down our unidentifiable food made by, I'm supposing, those unidentifiable hands. We go to the car in silence. As has been the theme, I cannot find reverse. Everyone is leaving around us. I can't get the car into reverse. Finally, the car in front of me and blocking my way forward, impatiently peels out and around the stick-shift car and into the night. I drive forward and around and out into the same night.

"I think I'm supposed to tell you something," I tell Susann.

"What?"

"I fulfilled a vow."

"Really." There is no inflection in the question. It very well could have been a statement. She doesn't ask what vow, or who might have told me to tell her.

"I saw the three horses above me."

"Really."

"I'm just supposed to tell you."

"Okay."

She says nothing more. I drive her back to Sam's and then to the apartment. I take a bath and imagine that sleep will never feel so good. I cannot sleep.

>>Dispatch: We Talk You Listen
The Next Day. 3:43 a.m.

I receive an email from someone I do not know who has heard about my work on this project.

As an American Indian . . . I find that it is important to have our stories told . . . but by our people . . . there are some things that non-Indians will not understand about us and our stories . . . non-Indians just need to know what we want them to know . . . I don't see any Indians trying to write a play about any European stories? . . . I also get tired of people who feel it is their destiny to have something done for the Indian . . . I personally would rather hear an orally told story by an Indian of any nation . . . I heard enough of the non-Indian stories . . .

Dang, why can't our people tell their own stories! Why do non-Indians feel they have to be the ones to tell the stories of a people they have no idea about . . .

>>Dispatch: Rage

Email to: Mr. Christopher Cartmill

Dear Sir,

A lawsuit will be filed for the use or misuse of my family name in your work. Here is what I propose to you—at this time I request the payment of $500.00 bi-weekly for the use of my family name. Are you willing to settle out of court? If so, you will agree to the payment requested above.

August 22, 2007, or thereabouts. Macy, Nebraska

Marc, a UNL student who'd volunteered to help me with some work up in Macy, is leaning down into the window of a large car, talking. He straightens up and the car peals out of the parking lot.

"What was that?"

"Some man that was really angry. He said that he was a descendant of Standing Bear and asked why didn't you talk to him. Who is Susann Cloud Horse or anybody else to be a gatekeeper for a story that's not theirs? I told him to stay, that you would want to talk to him, but he said he was too mad."

Chat Room Exchange about My Project

FROM "HISTORICAL VIEWPOINT," AUGUST 22, 12:53 A.M.

Your play sounds interesting but people need to remember when it comes to Native American history, what has been passed on from generation to generation has changed with each telling and is now not completely accurate. What is now called "history" is actually legends and stories.

That's your opinion Historical . . . and exactly that . . . just an opinion!! Obviously you are not a NATIVE . . . you are totally clueless . . . We tell YOU (non natives) just what you need to know . . ."

The email consists solely of a long poem of anger and empowerment. With lines such as: "You cram your culture down my throat / You fill my mind with a false sense of history . . ." Etc. I discover that the poem is not the writer's own, but lyrics to a piece by the mid-1990s alternative metal band, Rage Against the Machine. Good strong stuff. But, I think, if you're going to show me your rage—against the machine, against "the man," against the evils around you, against me—show me *your* rage, not borrowed rage.

Here's mine: Why have I given so much to a story I am not supposed to tell? By extension, I must question whether I am ever allowed to write of anyone that is, well, not myself. And as to the past and my place in it: What's the statute of limitations? What's the reparation? Tell me. I need to know because from the sum of these many considerations, I could very well be culpable. Some of my ancestors came to what they called the New World in the 1680s. Yes, and some went on to own slaves! But does that make me guilty? Tell me! Even if I tried, by myself I could never right such a terrible wrong! I'm good at what I do, but not *that* good. And, okay, get it *all* out there! At Cartmill's Gap in Virginia in 1757, both white settlers and Natives were killed in a fierce battle. It's never equal. It never will be. Does raging change it? It's also likely that as my Cartmill ancestors moved out west in the 1840s, they settled on more Native lands. Can we go back and explain it to them?

Can we go together? Get them to stop? What do you need me to do? Can I not be your friend? Should we just talk behind each other's back? Tell stories the other can't hear? When does it stop?

My great-great-grandmother! I know her name now: Mildred Lemon! She left the reservation and apparently rarely spoke of her past. Is that the pride and the shame? Can I take away what may have been her pain?

What if I choose to live differently, think differently? Stop the cycle? Step out of the wrong and away from the shouting match? Demand that the world around me be different? Reach out and across? Seek to understand and not just accept that I can't? Is that enough? No? Tell me. Say it! Like Rage Against the Machine did. But say it yourself. You write it. There is room enough. This is not *my* Nebraska, it is *our* Nebraska. So, please, write it in a play or a song or a poem or make a film and I will be in the first row to cheer you on. But sign your name to it proudly, and work very hard to make it as good as you can—not because you want attention and money but because the story or what you want to tell us is *that important*!

>>Dispatch: A Word from My Mother

A Letter Never Sent Found in a Notebook among Her Papers Just Before I Started this Journey

October 4, 1992

Dear Christopher,

It seems to me you have crammed many years, and much learning into the past year. You have accomplished an extraordinary number of important milestones toward your goals, but not without a great amount of pain and frustration. Often you have asked me why all these processes create so much agony when it seems so reasonable—so possible—so everything?? Unfortunately, I cannot answer the question even with a thirty year advance in experience.

Like you, many or most people I know, perceive all I do is easy. I guess the answer for me is I will go on working very hard, making it look easy, and hope to impact in whatever way I can.

Although there have been many times I have felt I was the only one lugging the large boulder up the hill, I went on doing it, as will you, because there is something to lug and there is a hill to climb—and just behind that hill another one and another one. If we are to do the whole range of things it is unending and requires stamina and staying power.

You have a singleness of purpose but a large case of humanity; therein is the rub! Humanity-sense will always rub you and cause you at least frustration, if not agony.

So many writers are eager to offer mankind up as awful, and lacking so much, we ask why are they/we allowed to exist? In all your plays you offer hope.

You tell us we all mean to do the proper thing and sometimes do it. You give us joy. You lace it with music, with laughter, with visual pleasure and with universal truths. You unite history with now. The problem is the world is estranged and reality may not exist. Certainly tv does nothing for mankind except to talk itself to boredom and list all which is impossible about mankind.

On this day of writing, I am especially proud of you because for me you stand very, very tall in bringing to the stage, and any media like it, the very, very important message—love is what we seek best of all.

>>Dispatch: A Visit Long Overdue

August 25, 2007

Alma Kisker, my mother's housekeeper and family friend, and her daughter, Deb Steinkolk (whom I have yet to see during this visit), have invited me to Alma's house in Cortland, Nebraska, for lunch. Cortland is a little town twenty-five miles south of Lincoln, population 488. Alma commuted for her once-or-twice-a-week duties for my mother for twenty-three years. When Deb was sick in the hospital last summer, Alma and her husband, George, took Deb's children to their home every day. As I turn down one of the eight streets of town—the one on which the Kiskers have made their home for almost forty years—I realize that I have never visited their home, even though this woman and her family have been an important part of my family—an important part of my mother's life.

The house is a well-kept Midwestern ranch built sometime in the late fifties. The pots of flowers out front dwarf the house. The lawn is impeccable. George comes to the door and Alma follows behind, then holds open the screen door to welcome me in.

The Kiskers are collectors—hardcore and inveterate collectors. This I had not known. At the door is a four-score collection of porcelain butterfly wind chimes. The walls are covered—truly and almost totally covered—with collectible plates. Floor-to-ceiling cabinets are filled with collectible figurines: Hummel, Royal Dalton, Lladró, Lenox, Precious Moments—you name it. Armies and armies of little figures, filed like little glazed soldiers of Xian. An extensive collection of Boston terrier figurines are mustered like battalions on the tops of some of the display cabinets. Even a side table is nothing less than a display center for faux-Dresden figurines in porcelain lace dresses. Strangely, there is not a sense so much of clutter as of repetition and precision. The room and even the whole house are not particularly large, but all available space is used and used well, mostly by figurines.

Seated in a light blue chair, surrounded by halos of collectible plates, is Deb. Deb has had some ups and downs since last summer. The most recent was a down month, but she is smiling widely and looking to hold court in her Wedgewood blue throne. She has the appearance of a sweet and fragile figurine. Carefully placed as she is on her chair, she gives only slight signs of the damage done by the multiple sclerosis.

"Mom, you should show Chris around! You want a tour?" asks Deb.

"Of course."

"You can already see we . . . collect things," Alma shrugs and snorts slightly. George nods and the two of them take me off into the seemingly never-ending maze of this tiny, collectibles-packed ranch house. "It calms us, collecting. You'd think we'd be pretty calm by now, wouldn't ya?"

It's clear that this has been a hard year for the Kiskers, what with Deb's illness and taking on the responsibility of Deb's two young boys. But they have not quailed from their commitment to getting through it and helping their child and grandchildren adjust to their new life. They are always encouraging Deb and celebrating her progress. Alma and George will say no more than that they're a little tired. It's understandable and understated. They've been caring for Deb's kids a good part of every week. Deb is doing much on her own, now, but she can't fully care for her children. This pains her. This pains her parents but they never show that pain to Deb.

The extended family is all gathered in the small collect-ibles-filled house. The older grandchildren are downstairs playing video games. Alma has been waiting to feed me. It's a fine collection of good Midwestern fare: Jello-One-Two-Three, brownie bake, barbequed beef, sweet corn, home-made sandwich buns, and "salads," which in fact are more Jello concoctions. Plus the Nebraska staple, Dorothy Lynch salad dressing, on iceberg lettuce. A casserole is in the oven. There's even more that I don't see or smell.

I ask, "What's the special occasion?"

"Tell Chris it's because he came to visit!" Deb's sister shouts from the living room.

"It's just what we do," says George. "Family."

Alma takes me into the kitchen.

"We wasn't goin' to eat till 4:30 or so, but because you gotta go back to Lincoln, I'll fix you a plate. Have you been eating well?"

I eat, gratefully, while Alma makes me a little brown bag. I do have to go. I go to sit with Deb and we make a plan to see one another next week, before I return to New York. She wants me to see her house. Everyone sees me out to the car—everyone but Deb, who stays in the Wedgewood blue chair. Alma and George keep waving as I drive for-ward along one of the eight streets of Cortland.

Is home the collection of our stuff? Is it the traditions? The food we share? Our memories of days gone by? All of these? None of them?

>>Dispatch: Of Families and Finding Reverse

August 23, 2007

Storm clouds move in almost every night. On Monday the sky gets the green-black that heralds tornados. The clouds let go with piercing rains. I can hear the tap of hail against the apartment's windows. FLASH. POP. I see the flash out of one of the north-facing windows. POP! And outside all the lights have gone out. The storm is shocking and beautiful and opens up to a dazzling sunset before a half an hour is gone.

I am invited to dinner with my best friend from high school, Guy Curtis. He and his family have an old farmhouse south of Lincoln. I drive up the long wooded gravel drive and catch a glimpse of the old white wood-framed house nestled in among the trees. Guy is standing on the porch waving me into a spot next to his car. I wave back that I can't make it since it would require going in reverse. He runs out into the rain, I roll down the window and explain.

Guy's dad used to be a well-known used-car dealer in town. Guy knows cars. Guy knows me. He says, "Just leave it right here and we'll worry about it later. Come on in."

Inside the decoration is warm, tasteful, comfortable, and inviting—unfussy attention to the littlest details. Thought, but no pretense. There's the old-fashioned yellow glow of light that causes, from the lonely country road that passes beyond the trees, many a passersby to wistfully think of home and welcome. The table is set well. Guy's kids are all standing around. It's clear they've been waiting for me.

Dinner is a laughing affair. I feel like the fun uncle with his fun brother and his fun family. Nothing is strained. Interest is interested. Jokes are lame and subtle. No one seems left out. Love is felt and expressed. This is family. This is what I've known. This is home. This, at the core, is what this whole journey is about. This is what the trial was about, wasn't it? For us *all* to be given a choice to find it where we are and where we wish to be.

Guy disappears as I'm saying my thank you's and good-byes. He drives up in the stick shift car after having turned it around. He gives me a hug and says, "Reverse. It's easy. Old car man's trick. Lift up on that little ring—right there under the knob—and bing, bang, boom. See."

Yes. It slips easily into reverse—as easily as shy hands into pants pockets. I know it's not an old trick. It's obvious and any idiot should have known or figured it out. But Guy is the sort that doesn't need me to know that. "Thanks."

"Buddy, thanks for tonight. I was telling the kids that tonight was going to give them a feeling of what my life was like at their age. It was. Drive safe."

"Now I will."

"See you soon." Beyond the gravel drive and out beyond the trees and fields the sky is ripped by sharp and crooked streaks of lightning.

>>Dispatch: Nine-Mile Prairie
August 26, 2007

Sunday, the next day, is bright blue and expansive. I spend the morning and early afternoon, dark and retreated, re-hearsing for my performance in Macy and doing a little writing and a little fretting. At 2:00 p.m. I get a call from Lib-by saying that Susann Cloud Horse, Dell, Libby's husband, and little Lillian, their daughter, are all headed out to Nine-

Mile Prairie for a walk and she asks if I would like to come along. They will come around at 4 p.m. to get me.

"Yes," I say to adventure. Though I am swimming in "no." Yes. No. Yes. No. Okay. I repeat Molly Bloom's last line from Joyce's *Ulysses* and relish the new context. "Yes I said yes I will Yes." I'll go. What's nine miles more? What's nine miles off the path?

Nine-Mile Prairie is, as its name suggests, nine miles outside of town—outside of Lincoln. Well, that was nine miles outside of town back when the place was named. The town is encroaching, and fast. Truly it has already encroached. Nine-Mile Prairie is on land owned by the university; it is used by UNL professors and researchers like Dell Bailey and their students. It's a giant lab and an artificial (if that's really the word) re-creation of native plains grassland—an attempt to reconstruct what that land and vegetation would have been like before settlement and cultivation.

Dell Bailey's SUV is full of energy as we drive out past strip malls, a McDonald's, and tract houses of expanding Lincoln. Dell is pleased to be able to show me the land—his prairie, as his daughter, Lillian, insists on calling it. Susann, in the passenger seat, is quiet and focused on thoughts that she is not interested in sharing. Lillian, on the other hand, is talkative. Almost immediately she asks me to test her from one of her car quiz books on spelling and object connection. Surprisingly enough the second word is. . . . f-a-m-i-l-y.

Next I am asked to proctor her search for household objects surreally placed in a jungle. I think she is testing me, not the other way around. She doesn't even have to look as she points to each fairly hidden pan and spoon. Lillian has sass and authority, but there is nothing precocious about her. She may be an only child. She is clearly intelligent without any of the drama or edge of the "gifted child" about her. As we drive out, while Lillian eats the remainder of her McNuggets and holds forth on random subjects, I think that she is not six or seven years old but more like a childlike twenty-six- or thirty-seven-year-old. Lillian was adopted from China, so I wonder about her home and this home and what she would make of my search.

The gate to the prairie is closed. Dell steps out and unlatches the padlock. Maybe it *is* his prairie. We drive up a gravel road along a chain-link fence. To the left are acres of undulating waves of high grasses. To the right are barren hills dotted with austere cement bunkers. Dell informs us that the bunkers are World War II–era installations; they are not part of the prairie but they give an ominous surrounding to this demi-paradise enclosed in chain-link.

We drive completely around the perimeter. Dell points out the lands that have been reclaimed. He tells us about the man whose house is visible just over and down a hill. Though attempts were made for years, the man was determined not to give up his land and home. The university wants the land to extend the prairie or resell it for development. The man just died in July. Dell is resigned that the university will buy it and develop it, not reclaim it for prairie. Dell teaches us how they do controlled burns in order to keep the land as much like a natural prairie as possible, approximating the natural cycle of fire and renewal. When they burn they have to be careful of the wind. A fire could easily get out of hand. Cedar trees almost completely encompass the whole place, like an organic chain-link. The annual prairie fires that once swept the plains would have cleared the trees. We park the SUV back at the gate and walk into the enclosure. Down the path we step out into the high grass—bluestem. Bluestem grasses once were native to and ubiquitous on Nebraska and the Great Plains. Shoulder-high and waving in the mellow, Sunday breeze. The tips are more purple than blue. We walk down the gravel road. Susann is still quiet. Lillian picks up pieces of grass and fallen leaves and throws them at me as we walk. She then giggles and runs up to get some more. Dell explains that this land will soon be truly endangered by surrounding development. He teaches us which grasses and flowers are native and which are non-native. Keeping it pristinely native is impossible. In among the waving bluestem are silver patches of native sage. Susann steps in to pick some. We all step deeper into the grasses. As we move into it, it gets higher—above my head, over six feet high. The wind is up and tossing my hair in with the bluestem.

"You're going to have to check for ticks when you get home," says Lillian as she passes me to take her father's hand. Dell has found something. We gather around and he shows us a rare prairie orchid. Really. A prairie orchid. I'd never thought there was such a thing.

Much of the land is peppered with little flags—Day-Glo orange or red, sometimes tattered white. These are studies and tests of the professors, researchers, and students. I consider that this is beautiful, yes, and artificial, yet it must be protected and surrounded by fence and cement sentinels and studied and prodded and probed and clearly marked native/non-native, indigenous/invasive. It's a perfect little lab experiment of what I've been experiencing. And I have to check for ticks when I get home.

Susann steps away into the grass. I walk over to her to get a sense of what she's experiencing. She is still quiet and taking it in and breathing it out like a prayer. I'm not going to press. I walk a little ways off and look to the east, over a gentle slope of gold and purple. The sun is hitting everything low and making gold of it. I finally take it in and breath it out like a prayer as well. As if on cue, from out of the high grass leap three deer—white tails up and trembling. They bound up and over the grass into a copse of the boundary cedar hedges. They were startled by me or by Lillian, who's giggling up on her father's shoulders and pointing in the opposite direction at something to the west. I alone see the three deer bound up and down and disappear into the woods.

We learn more that I have since forgotten. Back at the gate, after we've gotten back into the suv, we discover that the way out has been blocked by another larger suv. We drive back around the perimeter. We find a group of people looking out at the World War II installations. While Dell talks to them (in the hopes of getting them to move so we can leave) Susann steps out to gather more sage. It is close to sunset and Lillian has quieted down. The bluestem is still being tossed by the wind—breakers on a dry sea or summer spray on an inland ocean. While Dell is up on a hill with the others and Susann is just outside the van door picking sage, Lillian giggles and, to get my attention, says, "Look. Look, Chris. It's your mother!" I do look back. Lillian is squinting at me with mischief and then says with a strange soft care, "Made you look."

The people move their suv but before we leave we have to stop at the gate to the prairie. Susann asks to get out. She walks to a few yards away and stands for a long while with her back to us.

"Daddy, what's Susann doing?"

"She's praying, Lillian."

>>Dispatch: Of Prayer
Hastily that Afternoon

I park the stick shift car off a dirt road that edges the Missouri. It's the exact place where, a year ago, I took a series of twilight photos of Susann and her kids. I reverse the car into a nice dry spot, just because now I can—drive in reverse, that is. We get Susann's case out of the trunk. The case contains her eagle feathers, sacred pipe, and other important objects. Susann says we should go out by the river and make sure we can be unobserved. This seems too skulking and shameful for prayer. Susann tells me she doesn't want to be interrupted and that sometimes park officials or local police will stop participants in sacred ritual on the mistaken idea that the pipes must contain something other than tobacco. I tell her that for my Sweat Lodge experience I had read that the Sun Dance ritual was only made legal during the Carter administration in the 1970s.

"That's been the way with many Indian rituals."

This ritual of prayer is very personal for Susann and I only came to observe and am honored to be allowed to do so. Susann says that it is important always to pray: "Every action must be accompanied by prayer. But I'll tell you again that we shouldn't pray for ourselves, but always and only for others."

The Missouri River rushes along beside us. Susann prays for me, for her mother, for her children, for her ex-husband, for her family, for the Omaha Nation, for the Native community, for words that will transform, and she does not pray for herself. That will be mine to do. The leaves of three giant oaks surrounding us rustle in the wind. Susann hands me her sacred pipe. Holding the pipe, I pray in the way of my tradition, my ancestors, my people.

My father once told me it's best not to close your eyes in prayer. I never really asked him why. At that moment I could guess why. Four milk white butterflies fluttered around us. They light on the pipe and our faces and hair and then flutter up into the smoke of the pipe.

"Lord, give Susann strength and give those who hear open hearts."

Later that day, waiting for the car that will take me to the airport, I sit with the a friend at a coffee shop and read aloud some of what you are reading. When I'm done, we sit together in a momentary silence. My friend says, "It seems to me—don't you think?—in listening to what you've experienced—that everything has happened when it was supposed to."

>>Dispatch: New Vows

August 28, 2007. Returning to New York

The flight is smooth and uneventful. Last summer I kept asking, Who am I in this story? Who am I to add to what Chief Standing Bear said or didn't say so eloquently with his hand extended in a moment's silence? I'm still asking and now others are rightfully asking too. It's not a bad thing really. Not at all. Maybe there is or has been too little of that. It's all a part of the story, isn't it? The anger. The need to save. The failure to connect. The ownership. The stories. What's the next step? I will try to continue and see where it takes me. I can always stop. I will protect myself. I will stand up for myself. But I will not defend. I will hold tighter to those I love but I will sit at tables with people outside my tribe.

I've finished the first draft of a second play that two years ago I hadn't expected to write. I'm supposed to keep working and even work on the third play. I will make a new vow to be honest and try to live up to it. So . . . honestly . . . honestly . . . *I have no idea.* I may not have mastered the stick shift, but I am capable of going in reverse and I know what to do if I stall out.

>>DISPATCH: THE TRIP TO THE WARM COUNTRY
September 28, 2007. On the Way to Oklahoma

"With Standing Bear you've got to count on struggle," jokes Karen Fox, but she's only half-joking. She knows the energy that surrounds this story.

Karen has been trying to get her Standing Bear documentary off the ground for years. She is today heading down with a crew to do some shooting at the dedication of the Standing Bear Museum and Education Center in Ponca City, Oklahoma. She has generously invited me to come along even though this jaunt down to Oklahoma is on a small scraped-together budget.

A year ago Karen went to the NEA and PBS with her extensively researched script and detailed outline and was turned down for any funding. The powers-that-be questioned the universality of the story. Why were these events significant? How does this story matter now? Not accepting failure (something Karen is hard pressed to do), she has retooled the script. I can see the weight of it all on her now. Her allies and supporters are pressuring her for the story to have the slant they want: Standing Bear the Hero, Standing Bear the Civil Rights Activist. Karen is bringing a producer along. We are to pick her up in Kansas City.

Annie Marshall is a documentary filmmaker. She is part Lakota, in her late forties and a former Kansas City cop. Annie has the slouchy carefree cool of a teenage boy. She is dressed in cargo pants, cargo vest, and a well-loved base-ball cap. She rolls her own cigarettes. She and Karen do not know each other very well. I insist that Annie sit up front. We load up her things, which seem pretty much the contents of an entire apartment. The last thing in is her full desktop computer. As we start up the car she ties an eagle feather to the rear view mirror and we wave to her elderly mother, who has appeared up in the driveway. Annie drums on the dash and we're off.

I'm not needed. I recline in my leather lumbar-supported seat and watch the land I knew growing up pass by outside the window. Through the Flint Hills of Kansas we drive. It looks like the barren Scottish lowlands. Cattle dot a steeply rolling, treeless expanse. This is the landscape of my childhood. We pass Emporia, Kansas, where my parents dated and were wed. We turn off I-35 and head down Highway 77, which means we'll skip Wellington, Kansas, where I was born and where my father's parents are buried. We drive through Arkansas City, my mother's family's home place.

There's the old black train engine in the park, where we'd play when visiting. And what was once the old Wool-worth Store. I point out the bank that my grandfather ran. We see the house in which my mother told me her mother had taken ill. We see the hospital building on the old brick street where my grandmother later died on Halloween night, 1933. It all passes by so quickly and like so many frames of film. Karen reminds me that this is the place where Standing Bear and the other Ponca chiefs had their pictures taken on their first visit south. I see it all happening at once. I see how little separates us. I look back through the rear window—hoping to hold the moment—when it all connects: No now and then. No us and them. No yours and mine.

September 29, 2007. Ponca City, Oklahoma

The name, Oklahoma, is said to be from the Choctaw phrase "okla humma," which means "red people." Ask many Oklahomans now and they'll tell you it means "red dirt." They couldn't be more wrong and, to some, more Freudian in their slippage. Around 1866 or so a Choctaw chief by the name of Allen Wright suggested *Okla Humma* as the name for the Indian Territory—if not an Indian Nation, an Indian homeland, though certainly a made-up one. But at least it was something. What Wright and many others had hoped was for the U.S. Government to create an All-Indian State. But things being what they were, Reconstruction was a bigger deal and no Washington politician worthy of the name was thrilled with the idea of uniting the Native tribes. The Indian Wars had been all about divide and conquer.

Later, in 1905, the idea resurfaced, this time with a name change. The Sequoyah Constitutional Convention was held on Creek tribal lands. The convention was made up of leaders from the Five Civilized Tribes and others who had been packed off to the territory at various times from the 1830s to the 1880s. Are you ready? The Poncas, Cherokees, Choctaws, Pawnees, Osages, Tonkawas, Chickasaws, Seminoles, Kickapoos, Kiowas, Comanches, Apaches, Iowas, Sac Foxes, Otoe-Missouris, Shawnees, Eastern Shawnees, Potawatomis, Kaws, Creeks, Senecas, Cayugas, Madocs, Peorias, Wyandottes, Ottawas, Miamis, Arapahos, and Cheyennes. These would have been a considerable force, certainly, if united. The convention drafted a plan to make the eastern part of what's now Oklahoma into the State of Sequoyah. The convention's proposal was overwhelmingly supported in the territory and a delegation was sent to Washington to petition for statehood.

Well, as might be expected, the reception in Washington was a mite chilly at best. Seems the delegates weren't even given much more than a sweaty, fishy handshake and a "by your leave." Teddy Roosevelt himself was not particularly "bully" on the idea and did what he could to nix it. Like many interesting and grassroots plans in Washington, it was ignored into obscurity. It wasn't all for naught, though. The convention's work was used for the drafting of the Oklahoma State Constitution, ratified in 1907. (Standing Bear died in 1908.) But it was good and done for an All-Native State. Even though the thought of Oklahoma becoming a refuge in any way had ended back in 1893 with a glorified steeplechase.

You see, some farmers and cattlemen were getting annoyed by the Cherokees living on prime land that could be better used, they believed, as farmland or a throughway for cattle drives. Their annoyance was fueled by the fact that the Cherokees and many of their Native brethren had chosen poorly during the Civil War and had fought for the Confederacy. Not cool. A couple of times during the 1880s the government tried to buy the land, but the Cherokees refused. It seemed to be simply a matter of eminent domain and so it was only a matter of time.

The Oklahoma Land Rush (glamorized by Edna Ferber in the novel *Cimarron*) or Oklahoma Land Grab (unglamorous), was "Manifest Destiny" refigured into a kind of game/reality show. An area 58 miles wide by 225 miles long was opened to the contestants: nearly one hundred thousand of them. Perversely, the land was divided into forty-two thousand claims and each homesteader had to literally stake (put a stake with a white flag attached) his claim and then, with dispatch, go back and pick up a certificate at the starting place.

On your mark, get set, GO!

Watch with thrill and amusement as every desperate settler on foot, on horseback, or in a cart scrambles to stake a claim on the best piece of land, preferably near water—yippee-yi-yo! Land that had been once given as a consolation prize to Cherokees for completing the Trail of Tears.

I have in mind a picture from my high school American History class. It seemed so innocuous back then, and kind of sweet really—naive, like our elementary school years. My fifth grade teacher, Mrs. Teal, had a print of it on her bulletin board. I would study the picture then without really understanding it, taking in the lesson of power. I now know it was by a painter named John Gast. It is called *American Progress*. There's a giant strawberry-blond allegorical woman in a white angelic diaphaneity of silk. Her hair is down and rich with curls. She holds a book while she floats, chest proud and forward, above an expansive prairie landscape. *Columbia in excelsis Deo!* At her feet are settlers and a stagecoach, trailing behind her are telegraph wires and trains. Before her flee wild animals and Indians.

>>Dispatch: You Obviously Don't Know the Story

Afternoon of September 29, 2007. Main Street of Ponca City, Oklahoma

We park the car on Grand Avenue and step into a stumbling and happy sandwich shop. The walls are covered with posters of superheroes. This appears to be the popular lunch spot for all of Ponca City. We order our food, fill our soda cups that are as big as buckets, and go to a large circular table underneath posters of Hawkman, the Green Lantern, Robin, and a large and looming real-life Darth Vader suit. While we're eating a gentleman comes to our table to welcome us strangers to Ponca City. He is Jack P. Stanhope, the Chamber of Commerce personified, sixty or so, wiry, tanned and aggressively friendly. Behind him the Justice League of America meets in its secret lair. Jack P. Stanhope is the man who'd really made the Standing Bear Park and all the extras happen. He firmly shakes each hand around the table and sells the project while he investigates ours. He brings over a youngish Native woman and her non-Native husband. "This," he tells us, "is the daughter of the woman who inspired all that you're going to see. This is the daughter of Genevieve Pollack. It was her mother's courage. It's the courage of Standing Bear, you see. What do you all need to know about Standing Bear?"

Jack P. Stanhope may be a salesman but none of this is feigned or put on for a pitch. His sincerity beams over Genevieve's daughter, who is now shaking all our hands. Karen tells him of her mission, her documentary, and Jack promises that he will do everything he can to help. I chime in. "Sir, why do you think this story is important?"

Jack P. Stanhope looks at me as if I was the most surprisingly and pathetically ignorant child he has had the fortune of teaching about the ways of the world. He looks back with a furrowed and indulgent brow, then shakes his head. "You obviously don't know the story, or you wouldn't ask that."

Karen laughs out loud, but Jack P. Stanhope willfully ignores her.

"I wish I had my camera," says the NET cameraman.

"I've got mine," says Annie. She bags her tater tots and pulls out her camera.

I am not giving away anything. What *do* I know? And Jack P. Stanhope doesn't need to know what I know. I want to hear what he thinks. And he lets me know what he thinks as he launches into an animated, evangelical speech, detailing Standing Bear's journey from Nebraska to Oklahoma. He speaks movingly of the trial. It's all memorized. He even recites the final few lines from the famous courtroom oration. But here's the part that Annie's camera records and I note: Jack P. Stanhope gets the facts mixed up. It's memorized but slightly off. In his telling it is Standing Bear's daughter, Prairie Flower, who dies down in Oklahoma. Bright Eyes is completely missing for the trial and after. The chief goes on to be an activist for human rights until his death. But I'm not going to call Jack P. Stanhope out on this error. I want to know his Standing Bear. And his Standing Bear looks to fit with the superheroes that surround us.

"It's an important part of our history. It's an important part of Oklahoma history."

"But, sir, he didn't want to stay here."

He pulls back from me. He does not say something like "that's the point" or "how can you ask me such a thing?" Genevieve Pollack's daughter appears equally flummoxed. After looking confused for an instant, Jack P. Stanhope turns his shoulder on me and addresses an unasked and unrelated question from Karen. I'm a bad pupil. Mine was not, I suppose, a good Chamber of Commerce question. Who wouldn't want to stay in Ponca City, Oklahoma? And to Jack P. Stanhope, Standing Bear is *their* tourist attraction. You'd think he was eight and I'd told him Santa Claus did not exist. I was being inappropriate and cruelly ignorant.

Karen saves the moment with another question wrapped in flattery. I wish I were as good as she is. Karen has wit and finesse. Annie's got it on camera.

As our lunch breaks up, Karen is looking even more anxious and heavy-hearted. I apologize to her if I over-stepped, but she waves me off without really showing how generous she is with her work. She's holding to nothing. "But you can see how big this is. No one can even agree on the facts."

>>DISPATCH: COMMEMORATION
September 30, 2007. Ponca City, Oklahoma

"How many youngsters today know the story of Standing Bear outside of Oklahoma? Not too many. So my book—this book here—is coming out next April to tell the truth that I and others have put together! We want it to be known from "sea to shining sea" that this is a lesson in goodness and charity and courage between the races!" Such is part of a speech given by a former governor of Oklahoma on the day of the dedication of the Chief Standing Bear Museum. To my mind he gets many of the facts wrong. He refers to the trial as having taken place "nearby." He calls Bright Eyes an "Indian princess." He claims Standing Bear as an Oklahoma story. He calls T. H. Tibbles "Henry Peoples." He finishes with the announcement that he must leave for another engagement: a limo and box seats are waiting for him at an Oklahoma University football game.

Karen Fox is sitting on the ground next to me. She shakes her head. "It's all a jumble of what people want from this story—this figure. How can we capture that?"

"Yes. Because," I say, "if you listen, you cannot help but take it personally."

I watch as Karen interviews a Southern Ponca elder, Clare Rosemont, a woman in her eighties. She's dressed in an ivory doeskin beaded Indian dress. She primly adjusts herself in her chair. I sit on the ground, out of range of camera, to take notes and observe.

"But you know, it's like this fella told me, people are just sick and tired of Standing Bear, Standing Bear, Standing Bear from Nebraska. We should move on, they say. It should be like the story they told me at the Sun Dance. It was predicted that it was gonna happen seven generations after his death. I'm seeing it today. I have to thank God I'm still living to see unity coming. Four colors. At that Sun Dance, those are the colors we dance to. Black for Africa. Yellow for Asia. White for Europe. Red for America. Those are the four colors they were talking about. Every time they have a dance here, I've got so many folks that come from all over, they come to my home. I feed 'em. Put out a spread—give 'em a place to stay. I just got a small home, you know where it's at, but I always have room."

After a time, Karen looks over at me to see if there's any question I want to ask. "Ms. Rosemont, what's the Ponca word for home?"

"De-ta. It's your—it's your home. De-ta is your home."

I walk out alone to look up at the twenty-two-foot statue in the park. The towers of an oil refinery billow smoke into the sky. The wind is up.

To see it is odd. It makes him—a man—into an icon. And that seems odd to me because what strikes me so deeply about his story is that he is a person—a human being. Like me. To see him turned into this icon, this twenty-two-foot statue, is very strange. His story reminds me how much I don't know. Yet for a story to mean so much to so many people is extraordinary. People are astounded that they weren't taught it. The story seems to have things to say to everyone, Native and Non-native.

Am I doing it right? Am I getting it right? I wonder. But why does it matter so much? I guess it's because what is at stake is what it means to be an American. We live in a society in which we're all moving around, being thrown to the winds. And so what? Is home a place? They have built this incredibly beautiful park in a place Standing Bear didn't want to live. He wanted to go back home to Nebraska. Or did he? It was a promise to his son. But he might have wanted to return to his people in Oklahoma. He was a leader; he would not have willingly abandoned them. I don't think you can even contain this story in one simple telling because if you ask anybody about what they think or ask them to just tell the story, you get very different versions. That's a great story, isn't it? It's like a diamond, isn't it? Every way you look at it, it shines—and shows something you never expected.

But why is it important to me? I want to go home, too. Or maybe just have a home to go back to. This man is helping me find my way—helping me find my own way home.

I look up at the gesture of the statue, reaching up and out. It should be a challenge. Reaching out to demand to be seen. Not to plead. Reaching out to generations to come, saying, "I think a great many of you are my friends. Where do you come from? From the water? From the woods? Or from where? God made me, just as he made all of you, and God put me here—on this land. I see what he says to me: "Come! It's not done! We're all not home yet."

>>Final Dispatch: On the Road Home
Highway 77

My great-uncle Dick, in his late-eighties and my oldest living relative, comes down to drive me back up to the airport in Wichita for my return to New York. Uncle Dick asks me to drive and we talk about the past and the future. We drive back through the small town where my mother was raised. The sun is glowing low and magically on the stone and brick walls of Main Street. Uncle Dick looks over at me and asks, "Do you hear voices? How does it feel to be in your homeland?"

Willa Cather wrote: "The end is nothing, the road is all." Wherever you are, I hope you find your way. Safe home.